D0207971

Barbara Pym

a reference guide

Barbara Pym

a reference guide

D<small>ALE</small> S<small>ALWAK</small>

G.K. HALL &CO.
70 LINCOLN STREET, BOSTON, MASS.

First published 1991
by G.K. Hall & Co.
70 Lincoln Street
Boston, Massachusetts 02111

10 9 8 7 6 5 4 3 2 1

Library of Congress Cataloging-in-Publication Data

Salwak, Dale
    Barbara Pym: a reference guide / Dale Salwak.
      p. cm. – (A Reference guide to literature)
    Includes bibliographical references and index.
    ISBN 0-8161-9076-3
    1. Pym, Barbara – Bibliography. I. Title. II. Series
Z8721.4.S25   1991
[PR6066.Y58]
016.823'914 – dc20
                                     90-13044
                                     CIP

The paper used in this publication meets the minimum requirements of
American National Standard for Information Sciences – Permanence of
Paper for Printed Library Materials. ANSI Z39.48-1984.   ∞™
MANUFACTURED IN THE UNITED STATES OF AMERICA

For my son,
Ryan Patrick Salwak

The Author

Dale Salwak is professor of English at southern California's Citrus College. He was educated at Purdue University and then at the University of Southern California under a National Defense Education Act competitive fellowship program. His publications include literary studies of John Wain and A.J. Cronin; reference guides to Kingsley Amis, John Braine, A.J. Cronin, Carl Sandburg, and John Wain; and five collections: *Literary Voices: Interviews with Britain's "Angry Young Men," Mystery Voices: Interviews with British Mystery Writers, The Life and Work of Barbara Pym, Philip Larkin: The Man and His Work,* and *Kingsley Amis: In Life and Letters.* His study of Kingsley Amis, for which he was awarded a National Endowment for the Humanities grant in 1985, will be published in 1992 *(Kingsley Amis: Modern Novelist).* In 1987 Purdue University awarded him its Distinguished Alumnus Award.

Preface

Barbara Pym was a writer of distinctive qualities who, having suffered discouragement and neglect for fifteen years, was rediscovered toward the end of her life, to take her rightful place as a novelist of considerable originality and force. Pym's novels, often compared favorably with Jane Austen's, are essentially those of a private, solitary individual, employing precise social observation, understatement, and gentle irony in an oblique approach to such universal themes as the underlying loneliness and frustrations of life, culture as a force for corruption, love thwarted or satisfied, and the power of the ordinary to sustain and protect men and women who shelter themselves under it. The all-pervasive influence of the Anglican church, numerous references to anthropology and English literature, the weakness of men, realism, and a sometimes devastatingly comic tone are among the many distinctive features of her work.

The story of Pym's early achievements, her long-enforced silence, and her remarkable rediscovery perhaps says more about the publishing world than about either her books or her readers. Between 1949 and 1961, while working as an editorial assistant at the International African Institute, Pym wrote a novel every two years. As each manuscript was finished, she sent it off to Jonathan Cape. Her first six novels established her style, were politely received by reviewers, and enjoyed a following among a small but steady readership. F. Seymour Smith called *Some Tame Gazelle* "a quiet, charming novel [and] a comedy of distinction" (1953.5). Anne Duchêne would later call *Excellent Women* the "most felicitous" of all Pym's novels (1977.12); and Philip Larkin would regard *A Glass of Blessings* as the subtlest of all her books (1977.20). When *No Fond Return of Love* appeared, the *Times Literary Supplement*'s reviewer thought that this "subtle and penetrating" book confirmed Pym's place as "a witty chronicler of the shy and delicate"

(1961.1). In the United States, one reviewer called *Less Than Angels* "a quietly and consistently funny book" (1957.3).

Then, in 1963, Pym put her seventh novel, *An Unsuitable Attachment,* in the mail. Shortly after, it was returned: times, she was told, had changed. The "swinging sixties" had no place for her gently ironic comedies about unconventional middle-class people leading outwardly uneventful lives. "Novels like *An Unsuitable Attachment,* despite their qualities, are getting increasingly difficult to sell," wrote another publisher, while a third regretted that the novel was unsuitable for their list (1982.39).

Being a woman of determination and a certain modest confidence in herself, Pym went to work on an eighth novel, *The Sweet Dove Died,* which she sent off to Cape; it too came back. She adopted a pseudonym – "Tom Crampton" – because "it had a swinging air to it," but twenty publishers turned down the novel as too "cosy," too "trivial," too "clever," too "sad," too interested in the "ordinary" to appeal to modern readers (1984.54). Humiliated and frustrated, she began to feel not only that her new books were no good, but also that nothing she had ever written had been good. However, *No Fond Return of Love* was serialized by the British Broadcasting Corporation (BBC) and Portway Reprints reissued five others; her books retained their popularity among library borrowers; and Robert Smith published an appreciation of her work in the October 1971 issue of *Ariel.* But, despite these signs of the continuing appeal of her work, Pym could not find a publisher, and by the mid-1970s her name appeared to have been forgotten.

A renaissance in Pym's fortunes came with startling suddenness in 1977, when, to celebrate three-quarters of a century of existence, the *Times Literary Supplement* invited a number of well-known writers to name the most overrated and underrated novelists of the century. Both Philip Larkin and Lord David Cecil – for years her staunch admirers – selected Pym as the subject of too-long neglect, the only living writer to be so distinguished in the poll. Larkin praised her "unique eye and ear for the small poignancies and comedies of everyday life" (1977.19). Cecil called her early books "the finest examples of high comedy to have appeared in England" in this century (1977.8).

Not surprisingly, the publicity surrounding the article had positive effects on Pym's reputation. "In all of her writing," Larkin wrote of Pym in a longer article for the *Times Literary Supplement,* "I find a continual perceptive attention to detail which is a joy, and a steady background of rueful yet courageous acceptance of things" (1977.20). Praise of this order inspired much acclaim for the Pym novels of the 1950s and coincided with Macmillan's acceptance for publication of *Quartet in Autumn* in 1977; later it was shortlisted for the Booker Prize. Anne Duchêne found "the ties of consanguinity" between this novel and its predecessors very strong, though "the tone now is drier, more bleached" (1977.12). Cape began to reissue her early books; Penguin and Granada planned a series of paperbacks; she was widely interviewed; and she appeared on the radio program "Desert Island Discs" as well as in a television film called *Tea with Miss Pym*. When *The Sweet Dove Died* was published in 1978, the reviews recognized its brilliance and its modernity, though they did not quite acknowledge the extent of its difference from the earlier novels or the way the heroine both embodies and transforms the traits of earlier Pym heroines. Writing in *Newsweek*, Walter Clemons said, "*The Sweet Dove Died* is lethally funny and subtly, very pronouncedly sensual to a degree new in Pym's work. . . . Leonora's pride is pitilessly anatomized; her lonely elegance compels sympathy. This is a brilliant, perfect piece of work" (1979.6). Susannah Clapp, writing in the *Times Literary Supplement*, noted the "modernity" of the sexual themes, "a sudden lustful lunge by Humphrey . . . and versatile dalliance by James, who tangles first with a perky and eager girl, afterwards with a manipulative homosexual" (1978.19). Philip Howard called the book "deceptively simple" and said it was "sharp, funny and sad in its bitchy observations of these people living and partly living their lives of quiet desperation" (1978.31). Her last novel, the posthumously published *A Few Green Leaves* (1980), was praised on both sides of the Atlantic as "charming and funny" (1980.12), "beguilingly comic" (1980.15), and "magical" and "one of her best" (1980.28). The manuscript of *An Unsuitable Attachment* was found among her papers after her death and published in 1982 with an introduction written by Philip Larkin, who wrote of its "undiminished high spirits" (1982.39).

In 1984 Hazel Holt and Hilary Pym published a one-volume edition of Pym's diaries and letters, *A Very Private Eye*, which was heavily and mostly favorably reviewed. Penelope Lively for the *Sunday Telegraph* found in reading her life not only "the evolution of the Pym style" but the accumulation of material as the years passed. She predicted that "Pym addicts will be seized by this book; those resistant to the novels will find matter for reflection" (1984.69). This volume was followed by two posthumously published novels–*Crampton Hodnet* (1985), which she had written in the 1930s but never intended to publish, and *An Academic Question*, which she had written in two drafts (one in first person, another in third person), but abandoned to write *Quartet in Autumn*. In 1986 Hazel Holt published an amalgamation of these two drafts. In 1987 she edited a miscellany, *Civil to Strangers and Other Writings*, containing mostly fiction but some nonfiction. In 1990 she published her long-awaited biography, *A Lot to Ask: A Life of Barbara Pym*.

Since the 1970s there has been a flood of critical pieces, ever growing in quantity and quality. If there is a critical consensus, it is that Pym's novels are distinguished by an unobtrusive but perfectly controlled style, a concern with ordinary people and ordinary events, and a constant aim to be readable, to entertain in a world that is uniquely her own. Her novels are also distinguished by a low-key but nevertheless cutting treatment of assumptions of masculine superiority and other sexist notions, all this well in advance of the women's movement and without the rhetoric that mars so much feminist fiction. Although hers is a closed world – what Robert Smith called "an enchanted world of small felicities and small mishaps" (1971.1) – it is also real and varied in theme and setting, with its own laws of human conduct and values, its peculiar humor and pathos. Middle-aged or elderly ladies, middle-aged or elderly gentlemen, civil servants, clergymen, anthropologists and other academics – these are the people about whom Pym develops her stories. Some critics have felt that the narrowness of her life inevitably imposed limitations on her work. Beneath the calm surface of her novels, however, the events of the day do make an imprint, but to a degree appropriate to the lives of ordinary middle-class people. Each novel is a miniature work of art, distinguished by an air of assurance, an easy but formal control of the material, and an economy of means.

The world in which Pym's characters live, whether urban or provincial, is also a quiet world, evoked in such detail as to make the reader feel that the action could not possibly take place anywhere else. Taken together, her novels constitute that rare achievement: an independent fictional world, rooted in quotidian reality yet very much the creation of Barbara Pym. Central characters from one novel appear in passing or are briefly mentioned in another; delightfully minor characters turn up in unexpected places. This pleasure in cross-references is characteristic of Pym's art, in which formal dexterity and a marvelous sense of humor harmonize with a modest but unembarrassed moral vision. "I prefer to write about the kind of things I have experienced," Pym said, "and to put into my novels the kind of details that amuse me in the hope that others will share in this" (1977.1).

The selections that make up the body of this book begin with an anonymous review of *Some Tame Gazelle,* in the *Times Literary Supplement* (1950.1), and end with the American edition of Hazel Holt's biography (1991.2), published eleven years after her death. Between the two are more than 750 samplings of critical opinions, reflecting the fluctuations of the author's reputation in both Great Britain and the United States. A representative selection of critical comment drawn from newspapers, periodicals, journals, dissertations, and books has been compiled to achieve that purpose.

To increase the usefulness of this book, several editorial devices have been employed. Within each year, the materials themselves have been arranged alphabetically and numbered consecutively. Each item begins with a bibliographical reference that includes the critic's name (when known), the title and date of the publication in which the item is to be found, and the appropriate pages. References and cross-references are to those numbers (thus "1974.14" refers to the fourteenth entry for the year 1974). This code is employed within the text to refer to reprints and replies; it is also used in the index at the back of the guide. The index is inclusive, with authors, titles, and subjects interfiled. All annotations are descriptive, not evaluative. In the abstracts of interviews, bibliographies, major critical studies, and dissertations, I have emphasized scope, except in the case of very brief items.

This work owes much to many individuals. A major debt is to the compilers of earlier Pym bibliographies, including Judy Berndt (1986.10), Robert Emmet Long (1986.39), Jane Nardin (1985.50), and Lorna Peterson (1984.83), as well as the compilers of the Pym entries in the *MLA International Bibliographies*. I am also grateful to Constance Malloy, who shared with me the bibliography she had compiled while writing her doctoral dissertation; to Mildred Sharpsteen of the Hayden Memorial Library, Citrus College, who assisted me in gathering materials; to Margaret Cannon, Siobhan Bremner and Rupert Knox of Macmillan, London, for sending me xeroxed copies of several hundred British reviews; to Paul De Angelis, Caroline Press, and Jean Rawitt of E.P. Dutton, New York, for allowing me to study their publicity files on Barbara Pym; and to Hazel Holt and Hilary Walton for providing some early references. For helping to edit and proofread the various drafts of the typescript, my thanks to my wife, Patricia, and my parents, Stanley and Frances H. Salwak. Portions of my preface were previously published, and I am grateful to the editors for permission to reprint that material here (1983.58).

Writings by Barbara Pym

Some Tame Gazelle (1950, 1978, 1983)

Excellent Women (1952, 1978)

Jane and Prudence (1953, 1978, 1981)

Less Than Angels (1955, 1978, 1980)

A Glass of Blessings (1958, 1977, 1980)

No Fond Return of Love (1961, 1979, 1982)

Quartet in Autumn (1977, 1978)

The Sweet Dove Died (1978, 1979)

A Few Green Leaves (1980)

An Unsuitable Attachment (1982)

A Very Private Eye: An Autobiography in Diaries and Letters (1984; edited by Hazel Holt and Hilary Pym)

Crampton Hodnet (1985; edited by Hazel Holt)

An Academic Question (1986; edited by Hazel Holt)

Civil to Strangers and Other Writings (1987; edited by Hazel Holt)

Writings about Barbara Pym, 1950-1990

1950

1 ANON. "Women of Character." *Times Literary Supplement,* 7 July, p. 417.

    Review of *Some Tame Gazelle.* Calls this as "restrained" as its title suggests. The parody of a "literary" sermon is excellent; otherwise, "the book flows cheerfully on with little wit and much incident." Predicts that many readers will compare it unfavorably with the early novels of Angela Thirkell.

2 HALE, LIONEL. "New Novels." *Observer* (London), 14 May, p. 24.

    Review of *Some Tame Gazelle.* Says that Pym "creates a small well-bred Eden, but continues to insert a little old Adam as well."

3 JENKINS, ELIZABETH. "New Novels." *Guardian* (Manchester), 26 May, p. 19.

    Review of *Some Tame Gazelle.* Calls this "an enchanting book about village life, but no more to be described than a delicious taste or smell."

4 JOHNSON, PAMELA HANSFORD. "New Fiction." *Daily Telegraph* (London), 26 May, p. 24.

    Review of *Some Tame Gazelle.* "Miss Pym's sharp fresh fun is all her own. There is also an amiable air of scholarship about this novel which I find most pleasing."

5 WHITE, ANTONIA. "New Novels." *New Statesman and Nation* 64 (1 July):21-22.
> Review of *Some Tame Gazelle*. Calls Pym a "modest and original" writer who is "scrupulously fair" to her characters. Like a bottle of wine, this novel has "a bouquet of its own and more body than you might suspect from its lightness."

1952

1 ANON. "Divided Loyalties." *Times Literary Supplement,* 28 March, p. 217.
> Review of *Excellent Women*. Comments on Pym's humor and religion ("without much self-consciousness"), and finds here "a definite advance" on *Some Tame Gazelle*.

2 ANON. Review of *Excellent Women. Church Times* (Oxford), 16 May, p. 11.
> Review of *Excellent Women*. "This book reveals flashes of insight into female characters worthy of Jane Austen."

3 ANON. Review of *Excellent Women. Irish Times,* 15 March, p. 10.
> Review of *Excellent Women*. Says that "under a varnish of superb comedy . . . there lurks a most poignant tragedy."

4 BETJEMAN, JOHN. "New Fictions: In London SW1." *Daily Telegraph* (London), 14 March, p. 17.
> Review of *Excellent Women*. "Barbara Pym is a splendidly humorous writer. She knows her limitations and stays within them."

5 LASKI, MARGHANITA. "New Novels." *Observer* (London), 9 March, p. 19.
> Review of *Excellent Women*. "I don't think I've ever before recommended a novel as one that everybody will enjoy, and yet – even with a certain assurance – I'm prepared to vouch for *Excellent Women.*

6 LAWS, FREDERICK. Review of *Excellent Women. News Chronicle* (London), 7 March, p. 11.
> Review of *Excellent Women*. "We needn't bring Jane Austen into it, but Miss Pym is writing in a great tradition and knows it."

1953

1 ANON. "Family Failings." *Times Literary Supplement,* 2 October, p. 625.

    Review of *Jane and Prudence.* "Miss Pym writes well, and this chronicle of her heroine's doings is really very small beer indeed to have come from a brewery in which Oxford, a taste for Jane Austen, and an observant eye have all played their parts."

2 BLOOMFIELD, PAUL. Review of *Jane and Prudence. Guardian* (Manchester), 18 September, p. 19.

    Review of *Jane and Prudence.* "It is a horrid disappointment after *Excellent Women.* God and the Devil would never make over even the smallest English village, let alone suburb, to a set of miseducated nincompoops like the people in this tale."

3 H.,E. Review of *Jane and Prudence. Observer* (London), 20 September, p. 17.

    Review of *Jane and Prudence.* Calls the novel "too loose and rambling not to disappoint after *Excellent Women.*"

4 LAWS, FREDERICK. "Match-Making Comedy." *News Chronicle* (London), 9 September, p. 11.

    Review of *Jane and Prudence.* Calls this "a brilliant and charming novel, which you will not easily forget."

5 SMITH, F. SEYMOUR. "Novels." In *What Shall I Read Next?* Cambridge: Cambridge University Press, p. 98.

    Calls *Some Tame Gazelle* "a quiet, charming novel [and] a comedy of distinction."

1955

1 HOLLOWAY, DAVID. "With Rod and Gun in Far Suburbia: New Novels." *News Chronicle* (London), 3 November, p. 14.

    Review of *Less Than Angels.* "Miss Barbara Pym has a very keen eye for the tribal customs of the English middle class and a great ability for reporting them in a cool detached way."

2 THOMSON, GEORGE MALCOLM. "Love among the Primitives." *Standard* (London), 25 October, p. 19.

    Review of *Less Than Angels.* Refers to Pym's "gentle and unerring wit."

1957

1 ANON. "Fiction." *Kirkus Reviews* 25 (1 February):96.
      Review of *Less Than Angels*. "As a study of British tribal mores this has its moments, but the satire, if such it is, is hardly successful enough to give purpose to its events."

2 ANON. "Trouble Brewing." *Times Literary Supplement,* 18 November, p. 685.
      Review of *Less Than Angels*. Although the characters and events in this novel "are perhaps on the fanciful side of reality," Pym's "crisp dialogue is agreeably dry."

3 C., P. "Fiction." *San Francisco Chronicle,* 28 April, p. 23.
      Review of *Less Than Angels*. "In addition to showing a kind and warm humor toward her subjects – or objects – Miss Pym writes gracefully and shows a rare mastery of dialogue." This is "a quietly and consistently funny book."

4 FULLER, EDMUND. "Dark Men of the Dawn." *Saturday Review* 40 (1 June):14.
      Brief review of *Less Than Angels*.

      Pym is able to record her observations with "detached humor."

5 HUGHES, RILEY. "Books." *Catholic World* 185 (September):473.
      Review of *Less Than Angels*. Notes that Pym fondly mocks the anthropologists, but that "some well-directed malice would have served to pull [the novel] together more effectively."

6 MANSTEN, S.P. "Fiction." *Saturday Review* 40 (1 June):14.
      Review of *Less Than Angels*. Says that Pym's close connections with the world of anthropology is evident in this novel. She is able to record her observations with "detached humor."

7 NYREN, DOROTHY. "Fiction." *Library Journal* 82 (15 April):1068.
      Review of *Less Than Angels*. Calls this a "thoroughly satisfactory and gay novel" in which a lot happens. "The denouements of the several plots are surprising and convincing."

8 PIPPETT, AILEEN. "Observers Observed." *New York Times Book Review,* 31 March, p. 33.

Review of *Less Than Angels*. Calls the effect of this novel "curiously memorable." Pym's "sympathetic understanding" evokes from the reader a "chuckle for present complications" and a "sigh for supposed lost simplicities."

9 QUINN, MARY [ELLEN]. "Fiction." *Best Sellers* 17 (15 May):70.
    Brief review of *Less Than Angels*. Comments on the characterization, plot, and narrative voice.

10 WICKENDEN, DAN. "Fun among the Anthropologists." *New York Herald Tribune Book Review,* 5 May, p. 3.
    Review of *Less Than Angels*. Pym's introduction of death is as casual as E.M. Forster's. The influence of Jane Austen and Angela Thirkell is evident in her comedy about "the faculties of the dull or foolish or pompous."

1958

1 ANON. "Ways of Women." *Times Literary Supplement,* 23 May, p. 281.
    Review of *A Glass of Blessings*. Focuses on Pym's concern with the problems that plague married couples who have "failed to find each other, or themselves." Following her unsuccessful attempt at taking a lover, Wilmet Forsyth turns to religion instead. "This no doubt provides a more satisfactory solution."

2 GREENE, PETER. "New Fiction." *Daily Telegraph* (London), 14 April, p. 26.
    Review of *A Glass of Blessings*. Says that this novel surprised him. "[Pym's] naive heroine, all unawares, falls in love with an obvious homosexual (though this is never explicitly stated) and the queer goings-on of male housekeepers and so on are described with catty accuracy."

1961

1 ANON. "The Milieus of Love." *Times Literary Supplement,* 17 February, p. 108.
    Review of *No Fond Return of Love*. Finds here a good deal of "quiet amusement" as well as "subtle and penetrating" observations. The novel confirms Pym's place as "a witty chronicler of the shy and delicate."

1961

2 HUGH-JONES, SIRIOL. "Consolations for the Guilty." *Tattler,* 15 February, p. 13.

Review of *No Fond Return of Love.* "A delicious book, refreshing as mint tea, funny and sad, bitchy and tender-hearted, about what it is like to be a fading lady in her early thirties living in North London and trying to soothe the niggling pangs of disappointed love with hot milky drinks and sensible thinking. . . . I love and admire Miss Pym's pussycat wit and profoundly unsoppy kindliness, and we may leave the deeply peculiar, face-saving, gently tormented English middle classes safely in her hands."

1965

1 ETHRIDGE, JAMES M., and BARBARA KOPALA, eds. "Pym, Barbara (Mary Crampton) 1913-." In *Contemporary Authors: A Bio-Bibliographical Guide to Current Authors and Their Works.* Vols. 13-14. Detroit: Gale, p. 354.

Brief biographical overview.

1971

1 SMITH, ROBERT. "How Pleasant to Know Miss Pym." *Ariel* 2 (October):63-68.

Assesses Pym's publishing career between 1950 and 1961. Considers similarities to Jane Austen and comments on Pym's closed, enchanted world "of small felicities and small mishaps," her exact delineation of character, her "well-bred" form and style, her wit and sense of the ridiculous, and her treatment of religion and academe. Praises her first six published novels as "a valuable record of their time." Reprinted: 1987.44.

1975

1 KINSMAN, CLARE D., ed. "Pym, Barbara (Mary Crampton) 1913-." In *Contemporary Authors – Permanent Series: A Bio-Bibliographical Guide to Current Authors and Their Works.* Vol. 1. Detroit: Gale, p. 523.

Brief biographical overview.

1977

1 ADAMSON, LESLEY. "Rediscovered after Fourteen Years in the Wilderness." *Guardian* (Manchester), 14 September, p. 11.

Interview with Pym. Covers her reactions to being rediscovered, her writing of Quartet in Autumn, and her reading interests. Includes biographical background. "Her characters are often unattractive but always treated gently. . . . She has always found enough to write about in life as it is lived around her."

2 ANON. "Novel Notes." *Irish Press,* 22 December, p. 14.
   Brief review of *Quartet in Autumn.* Praises this "deliberately unfacile, uneccentric comedy."

3 ANON. "Points from Publishers." *Bookseller,* 24 September, p. 2168.
   Brief review of Pym's career before and after *Quartet in Autumn.*

4 ANON. "Six in Line for Top Literary Award." *Guardian* (London), 1 November, p. 5.
   Notice that *Quartet in Autumn* has been shortlisted for the Booker Prize.

5 BAILEY, PAUL. "A Novelist Rediscovered." *Observer* (London), 25 September, p. 25.
   Review of *Excellent Women, A Glass of Blessings,* and *Quartet in Autumn.* All three novels are sad comedies about "the small preoccupations of everyday life." In spite of its subject, *Quartet* – "an exquisite, even magnificent, work of art" – is not "gloomy in tone" because Pym never puts down her characters or dismisses them as old fools. The earlier novels are "assured and lightly balanced comedies." Notes the importance that the Church of England plays in her novels.

6 BAINBRIDGE, BERYL. "Books of the Year." *Observer* (London), 18 December, p. 21.
   Calls *Quartet in Autumn* "a beautifully sparse" account, both funny and sad.

7 BERTHOUD, ROGER. "How Are the Mighty Fallen – According to the Critics." *Times* (London), 22 January, p. 1.
   Notes that both Philip Larkin and Lord David Cecil cited Pym as one of the most underrated authors of the past seventy-five years (*see* 1977.8, 18). Mentions that Jonathan Cape might consider a reprint.

8 CECIL, LORD DAVID. "Reputations Revisited." *Times Literary Supplement,* 21 January, p. 66.
   Cites Pym as one of the most underrated authors of the past seventy-five years. "[Her] unpretentious, subtle, accomplished novels,

especially *Excellent Women* and *A Glass of Blessings,* are for me the finest examples of high comedy." (*See* 1977.7)

9 COOPER, JILLY. "Twenty-One Distinguished Contemporaries Select Their Favorite Reading of 1977." *Sunday Times* (London), 4 December, p. 33.

Names *Quartet in Autumn* as her favorite novel of the year. Although the comedy is bleaker and perhaps thinner than the earlier novels, finds here undiminished Pym's "compassion for human vanities" and "gift for the unexpected."

10 COOPER, WILLIAM. "Ending Up." *Daily Telegraph* (London), 6 October, p. 11.

Review of *Quartet in Autumn.* In spite of its feeling and characterization, the book doesn't make the reader want to read on. Larkin's verse arouses deeper emotions, but that may stem from the difference between poetry and prose.

11 DANIEL, MARGARET. "St. Luke's Summer." *Church Times* (London), 25 November, p. 14.

Review of *Excellent Women, A Glass of Blessings,* and *Quartet in Autumn.* Pym is able to make "ordinariness interesting and funny." Finds in *Quartet* a somber sense and a "more sophisticated, thematic approach."

12 DUCHÊNE, ANNE. "Brave Are the Lonely." *Times Literary Supplement,* 30 September, p. 1096.

Review of *Excellent Women, A Glass of Blessings,* and *Quartet in Autumn.* Notes Pym's expertise in loneliness and High Anglican comedy and her "marvellously acute" eye and ear. Calls *Excellent Women* the "most felicitous" of her books.

13 FIRTH, BRIAN. "Art of the Surface." *Tablet,* 5 November, p. 1062.

Review of *Quartet in Autumn.* Calls the novel "charming, mild, and deeply humane." Like Larkin, Pym writes with "an unpretentious stoicism and an unscornful but ironic view of man's potential." Because in this "small scale" novel there are no alternatives to loneliness, it is likely it will remain "something of a minority taste."

14 H., J. "Absorbing and Satisfying." *Evening News* (Lancashire), 3 December, p. 11.

Brief review of *Quartet in Autumn*. Finds the novel absorbing and satisfying because Pym observes her characters "so minutely and poignantly and with such tolerance."

15 HARVEY, ELIZABETH. "New Fiction." *Birmingham Post,* 23 September, p. 17.

Review of *Excellent Women* ("splendidly diverting and original character in the narrator"), *A Glass of Blessings,* and *Quartet in Autumn* ("as good as anything she has written"). Says that the essence of a Pym novel is "a specialized one of rich, cool placidity, laced with sharp but kindly satire." She is able to see beneath the day-to-day lives of her characters and transform what she finds into something "important and fascinating."

16 HUGHES, DAVID. "Fiction: A Personal Best of 1977." *Times Christmas Books* (London), 25 November, p. xxxi.

Calls *Quartet in Autumn* the "most ultimately refined" novel of the year.

17 KINROSS, RAY. "Fiction." *Evening Gazette* (Essex), 26 September, p. 12.

Brief review of *Quartet in Autumn*. "In Pym's hands this carefully conceived series of character studies unfolds with all the impact of a thriller."

18 LARKIN, PHILIP. "Books of the Year." *Observer* (London), 18 December, p. 21.

Quartet in Autumn differs from Pym's first six novels in its "macabre portrait of self-starving Marcia." Praises Pym's return, but says the general reader knows "she never really went away." (*See* 1977.7).

19 ____. "Reputations Revisited." *Times Literary Supplement,* 21 January, p. 66.

Cites Pym as one of the most underrated authors of the past seventy-five years. "She has a unique eye and ear for the small poignancies and comedies of everyday life."

20 ____. "The World of Barbara Pym." *Times Literary Supplement,* 11 March, p. 260.

Offers an overview of Pym's career and reputation and celebrates her distinctive qualities as a writer in her first six novels. Notes particularly "the underlying loneliness of life [and] the virtue of enduring this, the unpretentious adherence to the Church of England, the absence of self-pity, the scrupulousness of one's relations with others, the small blameless comforts." Finds in her novels the "deeper brilliance of established art; they are miniatures, perhaps, but they will not diminish." Excerpted: 1981.17.

21 LENTON, TIM. "Is This Life, or a Cheap Substitute?" *Church of England Newspaper,* 14 October, p. 23.

Review of *Quartet in Autumn.* Pym is "observant and sensitive to the nuances of a relationship; her writing is poignant and gently witty." Finds most poignant "the tragedy that life can be so small, so constricted."

22 MELLORS, JOHN. "Mixed Foursomes." *Listener* 98 (27 October):550.

Review of *Quartet in Autumn.* Against the intimations of immortality, each of Pym's four characters has a private defense: "resignation, religion, anger, and obsession to the point of madness." Hopes this novel will do for Pym what *Wide Sargasso Sea* did for Jean Rhys.

23 MOORE, ERNEST. "How Mundane and Compelling." *Lancashire Evening Post,* 12 November, p. 12.

Review of *Quartet in Autumn.* Pym's accuracy "makes one cringe at the tragedy of such empty lives," but all along the reader is compelled to get involved in their lives and by the end realizes that this is a gentle, loving comedy.

24 MOOREHEAD, CAROLINE. "How Barbara Pym Was Rediscovered after 16 Years Out in the Cold." *Times* (London), 14 September, p. 11.

The story of Pym and her rediscovery says more about her publishers than it does about her books. Includes biographical background and a report of Moorehead's visit with the author. "She is at her most acute, and gently funny, in a wry and infinitely tolerant way about people whose lonely lines are mitigated by good behaviour, a recognition of the true pleasures to be derived from small things, and the remote but ever present possibility that something good might happen after all."

25 MURRAY, ISOBEL. "Lonely Hearts." *Financial Times* (London), 22 September, p. 15.

Review of *Quartet in Autumn.* This novel shares with *Excellent Women* and *A Glass of Blessings* an "extraordinarily delicate irony, fine writing, understated humour and some bleak perceptions about the human condition." But the "more ambitious" *Quartet* is different because it lacks a narrator and offers a more obvious concern with the "darker sides of existence." But it is also a funny book, "keenly observant of the ridiculous as well as the pathetic in humanity."

26 OATES, QUENTIN. "Critics Corner." *Bookseller,* 12 November, p. 2891.
    Speculates that Philip Larkin may have supported *Quartet in Autumn* for the Booker Prize shortlist.

27 ROWSE, A.L. "Austen Mini?" *Punch* 273 (19 October):732-34.
    Review of *Excellent Women* and *A Glass of Blessings.* Praises Pym's subtleties. The reader cares about her characters and what happens to them. Suggests that she might be something of a contemporary Jane Austen because of her "quiet comedy, authentic and convincing." Excerpted:1980.24.

28 SHRAPNEL, NORMAN. "Tea and Sympathy." *Guardian* (London), 15 September, p. 18.
    Review of *Excellent Women, A Glass of Blessings,* and *Quartet in Autumn.* The earlier novels have "permanent value" and in their lightness underline the somber nature of her new book. "Gone are those earlier characters of indeterminate age, soliciting clergymen at church porches for vaguely benevolent purposes. Now they are at the receiving end, whether they like it or not."

29 SNOWMAN, DANIEL. "Britain: Self-Restraint." In *Britain and America: An Interpretation of Their Cultures 1945-1975.* New York: New York University Press, p. 121.
    Says that a fondness for "understatement, the double negative, the qualifying phrase, [and] the ability to try to keep calm under fire" all contributed to Pym's style.

30 SPRAY, CAMPBELL. "Dulling the Senses through Middle-Age." *Yorkshire Post,* 22 September, p. 13.
    Brief review of *Quartet in Autumn.* Finds this "quietly powerful tale" rather discomforting because of its subject.

31 STEWART, IAN. "Recent Fiction." *Illustrated London News* 265 (November):103-4.

Review of *Quartet in Autumn*. "In her amusing but perceptive novel Miss Pym reveals the quirkiness, the defensive and offensive mechanisms of the minds of those who are ageing and isolated."

32 SULLIVAN, MARY. "Sold into Servitude." *Sunday Telegraph* (London), 5 September, p. 14.

Review of *Quartet in Autumn*. Calls this rather disappointing. In spite of evidence of "demure rasping" that Pym's admirers look for, "the observations here tend to be unexpectedly spelled out."

33 SYKES, PETER. "Professional Mr. Fowles." *Oxford Times,* 7 October, p. 23.

Brief review of *Quartet in Autumn*. This will appeal to readers who enjoy "wry examination of life within a small social area."

34 TIRBUTT, SUSAN. "Autumn Sweetness for Barbara Pym." *Yorkshire Post,* 21 November, p. 19.

Interview in which Pym comments on *Quartet in Autumn,* her experiences with publishers, her attitude about the literary world, and her day-to-day life as a writer. Includes biographical background.

35 TOOMEY, PHILIPPA. "Novels." *Times* (London), 15 September, p. 18.

Review of *Quartet in Autumn*. Although full of "dark case histories and ultimately tragedy," this is by no means a sad book. Notes how far away the world in this novel seems from the world she created in *Excellent Women* and *A Glass of Blessings*.

36 TREGLOWN, JEREMY. "Puff Puff Puff." *New Statesman* 94 (23 September):418.

Review of *Quartet in Autumn*. The narrative point of view in *Excellent Women* and *A Glass of Blessings* "suffer[s] from having to maintain [Pym's] always rather prim, sentimental outlook." *Quartet in Autumn* is different; it is "impersonally narrated" and her characters' lives are "skilfully differentiated." Is pleased that for once Pym's characters "don't spend much time casting about for appropriate literary quotations."

37 WOOD, ANTHONY. "Right Back in Fickle Favour." *Oxford Mail,* 2 December, p. 7.

Interview with Pym in which she reflects on her feelings after being rejected by her publisher. Includes biographical background, her move to Finstock, and details about writing *Quartet in Autumn*.

38 WYNDHAM, FRANCIS. "The Gentle Power of Barbara Pym." *Sunday Times* (London), 18 September, p. 41.

Review of *Excellent Women, A Glass of Blessings,* and *Quartet in Autumn.* Notes an absence of the world's "reassuring quality of cosiness" in the latest novel—"a quietly powerful" book about obstinate individuals facing desperate situations. The first two novels, on the other hand, are "gently ironic, delicately touching comedies."

1978

1 ABLEMAN, PAUL. "Genteelism." *Spectator* 241 (8 July):26.

Review of *The Sweet Dove Died.* Pym's reputation is tarnished by the publication of this "slight romance, written in a virtually unbroken sequence of genteel clichés." Most of the prose is monotonous and the narrative is "deodorised," as if the "rude stuff of life were simply too coarse for [the heroine's] refined soul." With one exception—the issue of class—this novel lacks anything that concerns real people in the real world. Excerpted: 1978.47.

2 ACKROYD, PETER. "Minor Passions at a Good Address." *Sunday Times* (London), 16 July, p. 41.

Review of *The Sweet Dove Died.* Comments on the novel's mannerisms, vocabulary, and "conventionally coy omniscience." Says that Pym is too close to her material to be "a convincingly comic or perceptive novelist."

3 ANON. "Author Comes in from the Cold." *Eastern Times* (London), 25 May, p. 36.

Interview with Pym on the occasion of the publication of *The Sweet Dove Died.* Covers her writing habits, her reactions to being rejected and rediscovered, and her experience with writing *Quartet in Autumn* and *Sweet.*

4 ANON. "Fiction." *Booklist* 75 (15 May):1166.

Brief review of *Some Tame Gazelle.* "Pym is exquisitely charming as she pokes gentle fun at simple people's distress over small issues in life." Finds the book's theme refreshingly positive: "that despite upsets, regularity in one's existence can triumph and the future loom comfortably pat."

5 ANON. "Fiction." *Kirkus Reviews* 46 (15 July):773-74.
    Review of *Quartet in Autumn*. In this "terribly frank, but very affecting" novel, Pym never loses her respect or compassion for her "put-upon" characters, and as a result, neither does the reader. Her writing is economical as she cuts from scene to scene.

6 ANON. "Fiction." *Kirkus Reviews* 46 (1 August):837.
    Review of *Excellent Women*. "Though more cleanly crafted, more consistently dry in tone than the comic/pathetic *Quartet in Autumn*, this 25-year-old novel, dated but of too recent a vintage for nostalgic charm, is less accessible to a broad audience, more of a special treat for lovers of the high, wry style."

7 ANON. "Holiday Reading: Fiction." *Observer* (London), 23 July, p. 21.
    Cites *The Sweet Dove Died* as "assured and stylish, and often very funny." Pym's treatment is "cool and witty."

8 ANON. "Notable." *Time* 112 (9 October):114-15.
    Review of *Quartet in Autumn*. Into a quiet, ordinary situation Pym works "the subtlest of nuances [in this novel], endowing her characters with quiet dignity and endearing quirks." Her characters' "wise, rueful compassion" is rare in contemporary fiction.

9 ANON. "PW Forecasts: Fiction." *Publishers Weekly* 214 (24 July):78.
    Review of *Quartet in Autumn*. Calls Pym "pure gold." Running through this quiet portrait of four lives there is a melody of "beauty, dignity and spirit."

10 ANON. "PW Forecasts: Fiction." *Publishers Weekly* 214 (24 July):80.
    Brief review of *Excellent Women*. Pym's world is "a lonely, bittersweet familiar place. She travels it with rueful wit, views the human landscape with a wise, sharp, compassionate eye."

11 ANON. "*Quartet in Autumn:* A Touching Story of A Single Woman." *Denver Post*, 29 October, p. 13.
    Review of *Quartet in Autumn*. Calls this a "touching portrait" and an "intimate look at four eccentric, yet typical human people."

12 ANON. "The State of Fiction, a Symposium." *New Review* 5, no. 1:58, 74-5.
    Brief overview of Pym's career and reception by readers and reviewers. A.N. Wilson calls her "the patron saint of all whose work has been edited out of existence, or actually rejected, because of the

illiterate whims of some chain-smoking publisher or another." Pym comments on her favorite authors and the difficulty with selling novels. "I want the novel to flourish and to be highly regarded in *all* its various forms and to meet the needs of its enormous variety of readers."

13 BAUM, JOAN. "Excellence Rediscovered." *Newsday,* 1 October, p. 20.

Review of *Excellent Women* and *Quartet in Autumn.* "Pym brings understanding, cool wit and controlled affection to a group most literature passes by but which, by numbers alone, represents a growing portion of humanity."

14 BERKELEY, MIRIAM. "A 'Lost' Writer Restored." *Chicago Sunday Sun-Times,* 24 December, p. 44.

Review of *Excellent Women* and *Quartet in Autumn.* Finds in both novels the same "intelligence and deftly satirical touch." Pym knows her characters very well, and "what's so refreshing these days, she clearly cares about them in spite of their obvious foibles."

15 BOETH, RICHARD. "Brief Lives." *Newsweek* 92 (23 October):121.

Review of *Quartet in Autumn.* Pym is "a master of the precise and beautifully shaded miniature portrait." All of her writing is filled with "psychological insight and with the poignance of small, lonely, blameless lives." Her specialty is the assumptions that people make about others. Reading this novel, or any of her others, is a wonderful experience, "full of unduplicable perceptions, sensations and soul-stirrings."

16 BRODIE, POLLY. "Fiction." *Library Journal* 103 (15 October):2135-36.

Brief review of *Excellent Women* and *Quartet in Autumn.* In the former, Pym draws the protagonist's "emotional awakening" with insight, but the other characters are "colorless" and "the grey uneventfulness of the life portrayed infects the style." In the latter, Pym achieves "something of a tour de force, showing with wit and compassion, how ordinary quirky acts of impulsive kindness and human being make the difference between despair and hope."

17 BUTCHER, MARYVONNE. "Sympathies." *Tablet,* 2 September, pp. 848-49.

Review of *The Sweet Dove Died.* Calls the novel "wickedly sly, leaving the reader disturbingly unsure of just where [Pym's] sympathies lie, but in no uncertainty at all of her considerable talent." Comments on her "dry, prim" tone and her "faultless" satirical London backgrounds. "An ironic, unemphatic and highly entertaining novel tangential to the stream of contemporary fiction."

18 CHESMAN, ANDREA. "A Quartet of 'Nobodies' Brought to Life in Novel." *Rocky Mountain News,* 5 November, p. 12.

Review of *Quartet in Autumn.* In this "funny, sad, lonely, little book" the sympathetic characters come to life because of Pym's irony and eye for detail.

19 CLAPP, SUSANNAH. "Genteel Reminders." *Times Literary Supplement,* 7 July, p. 757.

Review of *The Sweet Dove Died.* Like many of Pym's meek heroines, Leonora proves herself capable of "acerbity as well as acquiescence." The momentum of this novel depends "not on the unwinding of individual actions, but on making the most of cosy moments and nasty little coincidences." Although Leonora is not likable, "it is one of the strengths of this graceful novel that her ability to make [her] points is not presented as being merely plucky." Notes, too, the "modernity" of the sexual themes. Excerpted: 1978.47; 1981.17.

20 COSH, MARY. "Dramatic Finale to an Oxford Quintet." *Glasgow Herald,* 16 July, p. 11.

Review of *The Sweet Dove Died.* "This quiet-toned book is insidiously clever in deployment of people and events." Pym's "deceptive sweetness" masks her "shrewd grasp" of her characters' weaknesses.

21 DOWLING, ELLEN. "Pym: A Twentieth Century Jane Austen." *Houston Chronicle,* 5 November, p. 22.

Review of *Excellent Women* ("painted with the delicate watercolors of Spring") and *Quartet in Autumn* ("displays the heavy oils and somber shadows of Fall"). The former is about "togetherness"; the latter is about "isolation and self-imposed alienation." "[Pym's] quiet, wry humor, her delicate affection for the little details of life ... and her bittersweet portraits of the Eleanor Rigbys of this world all make her re-discovery a fortunate and long-overdue literary event."

22 DUNCAN, SALLY. "The Two Lives of Miss Pym." *Oxford Times,* 26 May, p. 7.

Interview with Pym on the occasion of her retirement from the International African Society. Comments on her aspirations as a writer, her choice to remain single, her style, her reasons for writing *Quartet in Autumn,* and her sources for ideas. Includes biographical background.

23 F[LETCHER], C[ONNIE]. "Fiction." *Booklist* 75 (15 October):355.
   Brief review of *Excellent Women* and *Quartet in Autumn.* Notes a similar "vision and eloquence" in both novels. In the former, Pym understands "the wrestling of desire and emotion" within her characters. In the latter, her compassion is less obvious, leaving the novel "somewhat hollower." Although her manner is old-fashioned, Pym's writing is "neither quaint nor stuffy."

24 FRIED, ETHEL F. "Undiscovered and Unpretentious – Barbara Pym." *Goodtimes* (West Hartford, Conn.), 23 November, p. 6.
   Review of *Excellent Women* and *Quartet in Autumn.* Reading Pym is like drinking a fine new wine: "sparkling, delicate, unpretentious, with a tingling bite and agreeable aftertaste." Both novels are "quiet, precise, compelling, understated."

25 GLENDINNING, VICTORIA. "The Best High Comedy." *New York Times Book Review,* 24 December, p. 8.
   Review of *Excellent Women* and *Quartet in Autumn.* "Miss Pym's technique for comic effect [in *Excellent Women*] is to glide over the pain of big happenings and to make much of the disproportionate impact of tiny ones." In *Quartet in Autumn,* Pym "comes out" as she did not in the other novel; she tackles Marcia's "craziness" – what all solitary people fear – "wittily but head-on." Pym's female characters are "emotionally deprived," and it is in "the ironic exploration of the 'experience of not having' that Barbara Pym's art and originality lie." Excerpted: 1980.24.

26 GOLD, EDITH. "Books." *Miami Herald,* 3 September, p. 17.
   Review of *Excellent Women* and *Quartet in Autumn.* "Pym is a brilliant observer of life's ironies, and a marvelous, unsentimental chronicler of small events. Her excellent women and their old-fashioned friends are enchanting and unforgettable."

27 H., J. "Thoughts of Youth." *Evening News* (Lancashire), 17 July, p. 19.
   Brief review of *The Sweet Dove Died.* Praises this as "another quiet, inimitable story of human relationships." This "witty and observant" novel can only add to Pym's well-deserved reputation.

28 HAMILTON, CLEM. "*Excellent Women* by a Forgotten One." *Dayton Daily News,* 26 November, p. 13.

Review of *Excellent Women*. Comments on Pym's subtle sense of humor, "completely English, completely low-key." She writes "extraordinarily well."

29 HINERFELD, SUSAN SLOCUM. "Long Waiting Game." *St. Louis Globe-Democrat,* 16 September, p. 27.

Review of *Quartet in Autumn*. This quintessentially English book is "as spare as a Japanese print." Praises Pym's "smooth as silk" management of time and place, her "meticulous" style, and her "shrewd" observations.

30 HOSPITAL, JANETTE T. "Gallery of Eccentrics Is Deliciously Funny." *Boston Globe,* 8 October, p. 19.

Review of *Excellent Women* and *Quartet in Autumn*. An absence of much action in these novels would render them "almost stupefyingly boring." But viewed through Pym's commentary–"witty, ironic, delicate as fine old lace"–they offer an "unexpected delight." The reader comes away caring deeply about the characters. "They have dignity, and are capable of both triumphant and tragic moments." Above all, they are "deliciously funny."

31 HOWARD, PHILIP. "Fiction." *Times* (London), 6 July, p. 14.

Brief review of *The Sweet Dove Died*. "The book is sharp, funny and sad in its bitchy observations of these people living and partly living their lives of quiet desperation." Excerpted: 1978.47.

32 KENYON, JOHN. "Books of the Year." *Observer* (London), 17 December p. 33.

Cites the "enchanting" *The Sweet Dove Died* because it maintains Pym's previous level of achievement but shows an unexpected "capacity for development."

33 KING, FRANCIS. "Barbara Pym's Sunlit Garden." *Books and Bookmen* 23 (July):8-9.

Review of *The Sweet Dove Died* and *Quartet in Autumn*. The lesson to be learned from Pym's career "is that what, finally, matters to a writer's survival is not the inconstant tides of fashion, sweeping in and out, but the constant loyalty of a band of adherents, however small." *Quartet* is "beautifully-written [with] a marvellously sharp eye and a marvellously alert ear for social hypocrisies and self-deceptions," but given its somber subject, finds its effect to be depressing. In *Sweet,* on the other hand, the characters conscious "need to receive and, even more important, to give love" rescues the novel from gloom. Mentions *Excellent Women* and *A Glass of Blessings.*

34 KIRSCH, ROBERT. "Barbara Pym: Our Cup of Tea." *Los Angeles Times,* 16 October, pp. 4-5.
     Review of *Excellent Women* and *Quartet in Autumn.* Pym reports and re-creates her characters' world with "the cool fidelity and deceptively simple prose" of a twentieth-century Jane Austen. Finds in the latter novel "a maturation and mellowing" of Pym's skills. It is astonishing how much she is able to bring out of "seemingly unpromising material."

35 LANGLEY, ANDREW. "The Face in the Jar by the Door." *Bath & West Evening Chronicle,* 8 July, p. 10.
     Review of *The Sweet Dove Died.* Notes here a slightly "darker" vision, "more muted" humor, and "more refined" prose, but her subject matter is the same. Says that her touch is "exquisitely fine, for she manages to express her melancholy theme without losing her sharp sense of humour – as sharp and as finely tuned, at times, as Jane Austen."

36 LEIGHTON, BETTY. "Out of Obscurity, Two Unerringly Beautiful Novels." *Winston-Salem* (N.C.) *Journal,* 17 September, p. C4.
     Review of *Excellent Women* and *Quartet in Autumn.* Finds here Pym's most important theme: "life may impose hard circumstances on plain, simple folk, but there is a choice, not altogether unfulfilling – we can content ourselves with what may appear to 'the beautiful people' to be crumbs." Both novels have an abundance of wit and style, and like Jane Austen, Pym has portrayed within her small worlds "all humanity." Her characters are memorable.

37 LENHART, MARIA. "Quiet Novels Earn Belated Applause." *Christian Science Monitor,* 8 November, p. 18.
     Review of *Excellent Women* and *Quartet in Autumn.* Although the novels concern ordinary people in ordinary circumstances, "they succeed, in their own quiet way, in being anything but ordinary themselves." Neither novel will make "tidal waves in the publishing world or in the reader's mind; they are more like bubblings from a deep wellspring of human experience."

38 McMURTRY, LARRY. "Two Books of Barbara Pym – And Where's She Been?" *Washington Star,* 2 October, p. 22.

Review of *Excellent Women* and *Quartet in Autumn*. As a writer, Pym is perhaps "a bit too quiet for her own good." Underneath the comedy lives "a critical force." None of the characters "manages a fully satisfactory expression of any feeling." Pym exposes her characters' many "emotional constrictions," and perhaps the "quiet relentlessness" of this exposure helps to account for her neglect.

39 MASSIE, ALLAN. "Worlds of Spiritual Perversion." *Scotsman* (Edinburgh), 29 July, p. 15.
Review of *The Sweet Dove Died*. Finds this bittersweet comedy "elegant, amusing, a little poignant, a little unconvincing, but undeniably pleasant to read."

40 MEAGHER, CYNDI. "Pym's Novels: Showcases of Style." *Detroit News*, 5 November, p. F4.
Review of *Excellent Women* and *Quartet in Autumn*. Pym's novels are readable, humorous, romantic (without any sex), acutely observant of human behavior. Of the two, finds *Quartet in Autumn* a more serious and a bit duller book, but its structure and method are "awe-inspiring." The style and concerns in both books are "gentle," "unclamorous," and "elegantly simple."

41 MELLORS, JOHN. "Bad Trips." *Listener* 100 (17 August):223.
Review of *The Sweet Dove Died*. Calls the young men "somewhat shadowy" characters and Leonora "the product of sharp observation, sympathy without sentimentality, and a teasing wit."

42 MESHER, DAVID. "The Parakeats." *Jerusalem Post*, 4 August, p. 13.
Review of *The Sweet Dove Died*. This novel is concerned with love and possessiveness, with dignity and self-respect. Finds Leonora Eyre's development "convincing." The novel's success is due to "the distinctively British glibness of the narrative, the honesty and sensitivity of [Pym's] characterizations, and the courage to go beyond the easy ironies that present themselves near the end, in order to depict the resignation of middle-age."

43 MILLER, KARL. "Ladies in Distress." *New York Review of Books*, 9 November, pp. 24-25.
Review of *Excellent Women* and *Quartet in Autumn*. Mildred Lathbury is "shrewd and cool and self-possessed and stylish"; because she is without family and has friends about whom she isn't always enthusiastic, she qualifies for "the compassion which we extend to poor things, orphans of the storm." Like Jane Austen, Pym is a novelist of

manners "who writes about marriage and marriageability with the unromantic eye of a noticing 'positive' spinster." Like Austen, too, she is both "unromantic and romantic." But in *Quartet in Autumn* the imagination of "the victim, of the celibate, which has informed her fiction is less lively here, less hopeful." Concludes that these books come from "a very accomplished writer." Excerpted: 1980.24.

44 MOWBRAY, M. "Quartet in Autumn." *British Book News,* February, pp. 155-56.
    Review of *Quartet in Autumn.* "Quietly, undramatically, with an unerring eye for detail and a twinkling irony, the book describes the difficulties that elderly single people have in communicating, the prickliness, formalities and apathies that prevent them from helping each other as old age approaches." But surprisingly, this "engaging and truthful" book is not depressing; "poverty and the fear of incapacitation and death are, for the most part, tactfully avoided, and for this reason the book is slighter than it might have been."

45 NESBITT, W.J. "New Fiction." *Northern Echo* (London), 7 July, p. 13.
    Brief review of *The Sweet Dove Died.* Calls this a "delicate study" exact in its rendering.

46 OATES, JOYCE CAROL. "Two Rediscoveries." *Quest* 2 (November):78.
    Review of *Excellent Women* and *Quartet in Autumn.* Finds both novels appealing because of their "close, patient, sympathetic observation of small lives." Notes similarities between these two novels and William Trevor's "understated, gently satirical" novels, though Pym lacks his "depth and his ability to create characters who live in one's memory apart from the story in which they appear."

47 OATES, QUENTIN. "Critics Corner." *Bookseller,* 15 July, p. 266.
    Quotations from reviewers of *The Sweet Dove Died:* Ableman, Shrapnel, Howard, Maxwell, Treglown, Thwaite, Clapp. "It had, I suppose, to happen. The 'Barbara Pym Lives' movement had been so powerful last year that it was not surprising that when her next novel appeared there should be some clever dick declaring: 'It would have been kinder to have left Barbara Pym undiscovered'." Includes excerpts from 1978.1, 19, 31, 49, 51, 56, 58.

48 PAULIN, TOM. " 'Talkative Transparencies': Recent Fiction." *Encounter* 50 (January):72.

Review of *Quartet in Autumn*. Calls the novel "a bitterly amused account of decaying Englishness" that, like *Excellent Women* and *A Glass of Blessings,* is permeated by a "sad aroma." Her writing has now deepened into "a formal protest against the conditions both of life itself and of certain sad civilities that no longer make even the limited sense they once acknowledged." Excerpted: 1980.24.

49 SCOTT, MICHAEL MAXWELL. "Fiction." *Daily Telegraph* (London), 8 July, p. 11.

Review of *The Sweet Dove Died.* Calls the novel "delicious." Only Pym with her "scientist's cool eye [and] creator's affection" could breathe life into such a "monster of icy self-regard" as Leonora. Excerpted: 1978.47.

50 SEYMOUR-SMITH, MARTIN. "Small Is Good." *Financial Times* (London), 6 July, p. 37.

Review of *The Sweet Dove Died.* Praises this "slender but highly distinctive and – ultimately – charitable novel." This time Pym does not confine herself to exploring the conventional life; ultimately we are able to see Leonora Eyre as a sympathetic human being.

51 SHRAPNEL, NORMAN. "Unlike Curate." *Guardian* (Manchester), 6 July, p. 7.

Review of *The Sweet Dove Died.* "Miss Pym's steely grip on her creatures in this faultless novel is complete." Excerpted: 1978.47.

52 SOMERVILLE-LARGE, GILLIAN. "The Poon Show." *Irish Times,* 15 July, p. 17.

Review of *The Sweet Dove Died.* Calls this "a mannered comedy with tragic undertones," but is unable to make much of Pym's "peculiarly dainty humour."

53 STALEY, THOMAS F. "The Inside Story." *Tulsa Home and Garden,* December, p. 96.

Brief review of *Quartet in Autumn*. Calls this "one of the most poignant and sensitive human explorations" that he has read in a long time. "Quietly understated, subtly developed, Pym's novel brings these characters to a dignity and meaning that yields an almost uncanny understanding and vision of human feeling."

54 STEWART, IAN. "Recent Fiction." *Illustrated London News* 266 (September):103.

Review of *The Sweet Dove Died.* Calls this an "affecting study in miniature of the perils of deception." Although Pym's characters lack depth, the reader is "instantly absorbed in her fluent, direct narrative."

55 SULLIVAN, MARY. "Woman of Exquisite Taste." *Sunday Telegraph* (London), 9 June, p. 14.

Review of *The Sweet Dove Died.* Pym's "relentless observation" folds a great deal of "sly comment" into this small-scale, genteel, "demure account" of "utterly self-absorbed" characters.

56 THWAITE, ANTHONY. "Delicate Manoeuvres." *Observer* (London), 9 July, p. 25.

Review of *The Sweet Dove Died.* "The cool observation, the sardonic nuances, the style that dictates its own manner without quite becoming mannered, are all marks of this very original writer." Excerpted: 1978.47.

57 TOULSON, SHIRLEY. "The Sweet Dove Died." *British Book News,* October, p. 843.

Review of *The Sweet Dove Died.* "This latest novel can only enhance [Pym's] reputation as a writer of stylized dark comedies, whose ruthless compassion enables her to pierce the pretentious follies of the social scene and to entertain her readers with her penetrating observations of the ways and manners of the English middle class."

58 TREGLOWN, JEREMY. "Snob Story." *New Statesman* 96 (7 July):27.

Review of *The Sweet Dove Died.* Pym achieves "surprising pathos" in this "calculatedly thin-blooded" novel. The "memorable resonance," touches of high comedy, and satire have all been given more substance by Jane Austen and Elizabeth Bowen. Excerpted: 1978.47; 1980.24.

59 WADE, ROSALIND. "Quarterly Fiction Review." *Contemporary Review* 232 (January):45-46.

Review of the "brilliant comedy" in *Excellent Women,* the lack of "sharp-edged humor and cohesion" in *A Glass of Blessings,* and the often "uneven and fragmented" narrative in *Quartet in Autumn.* Comments on Pym's depiction of the social and spiritual life during the 1950s and 1960s and the "insidious and catastrophic change in social conditions."

60 WAUGH, AUBERON. "Approaching Height of Novelist's Art!" *New Statesman* 96 (26 August):13.

Reprint of 1978.61.

61 _____. "Have a Holiday with Miss Pym." *Standard* (London), 15 August, p. 22.

Review of *The Sweet Dove Died*. All of Pym's characters are silly, and many of them are odious, but "as the full extent of [Leonora Eyre's] ruthless selfishness becomes apparent, one finds that irritations with Miss Pym's mannered style and precious habits begins to give way to admiration." By the end of this "excellent" book the reader even begins to feel pity for Leonora. Pym's world is the world of E.P. Benson's *Lucia*, "where nothing improper ever happens." Reprinted: 1978.60.

62 WAX, JUDITH. "Two British Novelists Who Travel Well." *Chicago Tribune Book World*, 1 October, p. 3.

Review of *Excellent Women* ("gentle irony and unself-pitying acceptance") and *Quartet in Autumn* ("beautifully composed and the most pungent" since Muriel Spark's *Memento Mori*.) Pym's eye, style, comedic sense, and sensibility make inevitable a comparison with Jane Austen. "Barbara Pym's gift is that she can convey [her characters' quirky nobility of human tenaciousness] with such poignant, yet unsentimental humor."

1979

1 ANON. "Fiction." *Kirkus Reviews* 47 (1 January):31.
Brief review of *The Sweet Dove Died*.

2 ANON. "PW Forecasts: Additional Listings." *Publishers Weekly* 215 (12 March):65-66.
Review of *The Sweet Dove Died*. "Pym's extraordinary vision of an ordinary world wherein she details the intricacies of loneliness, the ditherings of hesitating souls, the comedies of errors, sexual and asexual, makes this a little masterpiece."

3 BLOM, J.M., and L.R. LEAVIS. "Current Literature, 1978." *English Studies* 60 (November):628.
Review of *The Sweet Dove Died*. In spite of Pym's powers of observation and her wit, she depicts "an intrinsically uninteresting set of characters."

4 BRODIE, POLLY. "Fiction." *Library Journal* 104 (15 March):754.

Review of *The Sweet Dove Died.* In Leonora Eyre's story, notes echoes of *Fidelio* and *Jane Eyre.* Her inability to love or be loved forces an examination of the reader's own heart.

5 B[UTSCHER], E[UGENE]. "Fiction." *Booklist* 75 (15 April):1275.
   Review of *The Sweet Dove Died.* "Pym's self-centered world . . . is too constricting to admit much emotional interest on the reader's part." Finds praiseworthy her "marvelously direct style."

6 CLEMONS, WALTER. "The Pleasures of Miss Pym." *Newsweek* 93 (16 April):90-91.
   Review of *The Sweet Dove Died.* Calls this "lethally funny and subtly, very pronouncedly sensual to a degree new in Pym's work." This "brilliant, perfect piece of work" shows that her boldness as a writer is growing.

7 COLE, THOMAS. "A Pym's Cup That Runneth Over with Wit and Satire." *Baltimore Sun,* 26 August, p. 21.
   Review of *The Sweet Dove Died.* "Gone are the more detailed and leisurely satirical probings" of the earlier books. Pym's prose is "highly controlled" and reaches "a most delicious and romantic ending."

8 DAEMON, R.F. "The English Way of Life." *Women's Week,* 5 March, p. 18.
   Review of *Excellent Women.* Praises this as a quiet book, a "gem of a novel," its tone "restrained, calm, delicate [and] decidedly English." Reading it is like spending time with a close friend: "well-spent, enriching in a peculiar, calming way."

9 DARYL, ANDREA. "Books in Brief." *Los Angeles Herald-Examiner,* 2 September, p. F6.
   Brief review of *The Sweet Dove Died.* Praises Pym's ironic wit and "sharp writing style" in this satirical novel about the lives and loves of a British antique collector. "Pym's characters discover they can only blame themselves for their destructive and depressing relationships."

10 DOWLING, ELLEN. "Pym: Silence Well Used." *Houston Chronicle,* 17 June, p. 20.
   Review of *The Sweet Dove Died.* To write this "wonderfully witty" minor masterpiece, Pym has obviously spent her "silence" wisely, "observing and listening to people so well that she is able to capture the smallest nuances with a sure and skillful hand." Praises

Pym for knowing "the precise word, the exact image, the perfect turn of phrase for each of her characters."

11 DULAC, ALICIA. "Fiction." *Best Sellers* 39 (July):121.
Brief review of *The Sweet Dove Died.* Finds it almost incredible that a "delicious and delightful" story such as this could be written "so smoothly" with the characters "so sharply alive."

12 GILMAN, JAYNE. "Miss Pym Wields a Fine Brush So Skilfully." *Oxford Mail,* 6 July, p. 11.
Review of *The Sweet Dove Died.* Notes Pym's subtle characterizations in this "beautifully written" novel with which she manipulates the reader's feelings with "consummate skill."

13 HINERFELD, SUSAN SLOCUM. "A Case of Possessions." *St. Louis Globe-Democrat,* 19-20 May, p. 17.
Review of *The Sweet Dove Died.* Reads this novel as "a wonder of miniaturization and compression" about romance, modern economics, unhappiness, and the human heart.

14 LEIGHTON, BETTY. "Stead and Pym's Revival Is a Cause for Rejoicing." *Winston-Salem* (N.C.) *Journal,* 13 May, p. 17.
Review of *The Sweet Dove Died.* Finds it difficult to describe the plot of a Pym novel. Her characters' limited small lives sound, in summation, "anything but compelling." Only by reading the novel can the plot be appreciated. "Pym, a careful observer of humanity, as is any great writer, has an absolutely steel grasp on her subject matter. Her books resonate with life."

15 LONG, GRADY. "The Long View." *Chattanooga Times,* 11 March, p. 13.
Review of *Quartet in Autumn.* Calls this "a novel of great substance"; after the first two pages, the reader is hooked. Pym writes with wry humor, compassion, and simplicity. "It has been a long time since I have encountered such superb handling of dialogue."

16 McMURTRY, LARRY. "Artistic Return for Barbara Pym." *Washington Star,* 27 May, p. 26.
Review of *The Sweet Dove Died.* In this "precise, lucid" novel Pym is writing at the "top of her powers" about the "unlived life." Notes similarities between Leonora and Strether, the hero of Henry James's *The Ambassadors.*

17 MADDOCKS, MELVIN. " 'I Don't Need Anybody,' and Other Illusions." *Christian Science Monitor,* 5 March, p. 27.

   In a discussion of loneliness mentions *Quartet in Autumn* – in which Pym has "delicately shaded the nuances of retreat that occur when people who have never been very engaged retire."

18 MEAGHER, CYNDI. "Pym's Wicked Wit Carves Another Gem." *Detroit News,* 15 April, p. 19.

   Review of *The Sweet Dove Died.* This "exquisitely detailed, elegantly worked" psychological novel plays on the theme of "the difference between the way one sees oneself and the way one is seen by others." Lacks the "romantic suspense" of *Excellent Women* and the "important concerns" of *Quartet in Autumn,* but its "excellence" provides pleasure and its wit is "delightfully wicked."

19 MODERT, JO. "Book Reviews." *St. Louis Post-Dispatch,* 1 May, p. 13.

   Review of *The Sweet Dove Died.* Says that Pym owes more to Charlotte Brontë than to Jane Austen, whose "touch of high comedy" she lacks. Compares this novel to *Excellent Women* and *Quartet in Autumn.*

20 OVERMYER, JANET. " 'Sensible People' Shine in Barbara Pym Novels." *Columbus Dispatch,* 1 April, p. 21.

   Review of *Excellent Women* and *Quartet in Autumn.* We come away knowing Pym's characters better than we know our friends. This superb novelist has a "quiet yet sharp sense of humor."

21 PINKHAM, PENNY. "Pym's Latest Missing Something." *Boston Globe,* 24 June, p. 91.

   Review of *The Sweet Dove Died.* In spite of Pym's rare skills and intelligence, her ironic distance robs the book of "the power of its execution. We are peering through an ironic prism, somehow bereft of the light source that would let it blaze away." Finds suggestions here of Muriel Spark, but without her driving sense of absurdity.

22 ROSENSTEIN, HARRIET. "Have You Discovered Barbara Pym Yet?" *Ms.* 7 (May):33-35.

   Review of *Excellent Women, Quartet in Autumn,* and *The Sweet Dove Died.* Finds in all three books "astonishingly good" prose. The plot line in *Excellent Women* "moves with such wit and verse that it takes a while to recognize how deeply unfunny the novel is at heart." The narrative voice in *Quartet in Autumn* is "simpler than ever, ironic, alert to the ridiculous, but uncannily rich." *The Sweet Dove Died* is "virtually flawless: witty, perfectly constructed, without an extra ounce of verbiage." Ends by praising Pym's "intelligence and feeling for the experience of solitary women."

23 RUBINS, JOSH. "The Browser." *Harvard Magazine,* January/February, p. 65.

Discusses the influence that book reviewers have on the success (or failure) of certain novels, using *Excellent Women* and *Quartet in Autumn* as examples. No amount of "rigorous criticism," no expensive "show-biz paraphernalia" is needed to keep a book alive, as long as a few thousand copies are "out and around in libraries and bookstores; . . . all it takes is one reader to pick it up and start turning pages."

24 SPRAY, CAMPBELL. "A Tiresome Tale, Superbly Told." *Yorkshire Post,* 6 July, p. 23.

Review of *The Sweet Dove Died.* Comments on the pretentious characters and their privileged lives. "They are found brittle and wanting, especially when compared with Phoebe, the one person in the book who lacks style, but certainly has passion."

25 STALEY, THOMAS F. "The Inside Story." *Tulsa Home and Garden,* March, pp. 76-77.

Review of *Excellent Women.* Although Pym's range is on a much smaller scale than Jane Austen's, her work is "no less real and penetrating." Praises this novel for its "deft touches, wry wit, subtle prose," and characterization. Her prose gives "depth and meaning" to her characters.

26 TEHAN, ARLINE B. "Artistic." *Hartford* (Conn.) *Courant,* 29 April, p. 14.

Review of *The Sweet Dove Died.* Each scene is constructed like a well-made play in this "cleverly crafted" novel.

27 TOULSON, SHIRLEY. "Barbara Pym." *Ulster Tatler* 32 (January):32-33.

Offers an overview of Pym's career: her reputation, themes, style, and favorite authors. She sharpens the reader's senses "by her acute response to the small habits and quirks of behaviour, which signal fundamental human motives and purposes."

28 UPDIKE, JOHN. "Books: Lem and Pym." *New Yorker* 55 (26 February):116-21.

Review of *Excellent Women* and *Quartet in Autumn*. The former is "a startling reminder that solitude may be chosen, and that a lively, full novel can be constructed within the precincts of that regressive virtue, feminine patience." The latter is "a marvel of fictional harmonics, a beautifully calm and rounded passage in and out of four isolated individuals." Notes parallels between the worlds of Pym and Stanislaw Lem. Reprinted: 1983.66.

1980

1 ANON. "Announcement." *Kirkus Reviews* 48 (1 December):1544.
    In *Less Than Angels* finds Pym to be "ironic, shrewd, a bit sad." Her story offers a wider range of activity, and the women offer "a bit more variety than usual."

2 ANON. "Barbara Pym." *Times* (London), 5 May, p. C10.
    Summarizes the contents of Pym's will.

3 ANON. "Fiction." *Kirkus Reviews* 48 (15 February):249.
    Review of *A Glass of Blessings*. Calls this comedy "a bit less coldly dry than *Excellent Women* though still not as emotionally affecting as *Quartet in Autumn*."

4 ANON. "Fiction." *Kirkus Reviews* 48 (15 July):933.
    Review of *A Few Green Leaves*. Calls Emma Howick a "half-sketched heroine," but finds "real, modest achievement ... in the accumulation of tiny, touching, ironic observations and reflections." Lacks the "smiling, sharp edges" of her early novels and the "perfectly controlled pathos" of *Quartet in Autumn*.

5 ANON. "Obituary: Miss Barbara Pym – Novelist of Distinctive Qualities." *Times* (London), 14 January, p. 14.
    Obituary notice with biographical background. Calls her a novelist of "considerable originality."

6 ANON. "Obituary Notes." *Publishers Weekly* 217 (14 March):16.
    Brief obituary notice.

7 ANON. "Paperbacks: New and Noteworthy." *New York Times Book Review*, 31 August, p. 19.
    Brief review of *Excellent Women, Quartet in Autumn*, and *The Sweet Dove Died*. Refers to Pym's reputation for her "ironic explorations of the experience of not having."

8 ANON. "PW Forecasts: Fiction." *Publishers Weekly* 218 (29 August):355.

Review of *A Few Green Leaves*. "Pym etches a miniature portrait of an Oxfordshire village caught between past and present, people with interesting and exasperating 'characters.'" Calls Pym a "gentle chronicler of small events."

9 ANON. "PW Forecasts: Fiction." *Publishers Weekly* 218 (5 December):43.

Review of *Less Than Angels*. This "top-drawer" novel provokes "amusement and wonder." Catherine Oliphant and Tom Mallow are "strangely real."

10 ANON. "Pym, Barbara (Mary Crampton)." In *World Authors 1970-1975*. Edited by John Wakeman. New York: H.W. Wilson, pp. 663-66.

Overview of Pym's life, work, and critical reputation. Includes autobiographical statement and discussion of the themes, characters, and style in her first eight novels.

11 ANON. "The Top Shelf." *Chicago Tribune Book World,* 13 January, p. 7.

Brief review of *The Sweet Dove Died*. Calls this "an elegant comedy of amorous cross-purposes." Pym's novels are likely to enchant readers of Muriel Spark, Henry James, and Jane Austen.

12 ANON. "The Top Shelf." *Chicago Tribune Book World,* 3 August, p. 5.

Review of *A Glass of Blessings*. Notes similarities between this "charming and funny" comedy of manners and the writings of Mrs. Gaskell.

13 AUER, MARILYN. "Women's Roles Spark New Novels." *Milwaukee Journal,* 8 May, p. 16.

Brief review of *Jane and Prudence*. Although the action seems "relatively leisurely" and the characters "somewhat naïve," finds validity in the characterization and skill in the writing.

14 BAILEY, HILARY. "Gone with the Wind and Company." *Guardian* (Manchester), 17 July, p. 21.

Review of *A Few Green Leaves*. Like so many contemporary novels, this one is "biography or autobiography but there is no transforming imagination." Excerpted: 1980.60.

15 BAILEY, PAUL. "The Art of the Ordinary." *Observer* (London), 27 July, p. 29.
   Review of *A Few Green Leaves.* Recommends the novel for the "quiet confidence of its unhurried narrative, which accommodates a dozen or so sharply differentiated characters in a beguilingly comic manner."

16 BAIRD, MICHELE ROSS. "Writer Barbara Pym Knew That Real Life Is Enough." *Atlanta Journal,* 11 May, p. 13.
   Brief review of *A Glass of Blessings.*

17 BARGREEN, MELINDA. "Fiction." *Seattle Times Magazine,* 22 June, p. 12.
   Review of *A Glass of Blessings.* "Nobody escapes Pym's narrowed eye, but her observations are never merely destructive." Finds that all of her novels are "witty, pungent, and wryly written."

18 BAWDEN, NINA. "Recent Fiction." *Daily Telegraph* (London), 17 July, p. 3.
   Review of *A Few Green Leaves.* Pym writes "agreeably, in nice, clear prose, and even if the people she writes about are fictionally conventional [and thus reminiscent more of Agatha Christie than Jane Austen], she observes them with a careful, mannered irony." Excerpted: 1980.60.

19 BILLINGTON, RACHEL. "Spinster Spy." *Financial Times* (London), 2 August, p. 15.
   Review of *A Few Green Leaves.* Finds here a conventional moral code that gives to her writing a "strong backbone." Her strong sense of humor diverts attention away from a "lack of vitality" and characterization that is "thinner than usual."

20 BRAINE, JOHN. "Truth for Writing's Sake." *Sunday Telegraph* (London), 3 August, p. 11.
   Review of *A Few Green Leaves.* While admitting Pym's skill, deftness, and delicacy, calls Pym's world a "dream world [that is] much too cosy, much too quiet, much too muted, much too safe." Her characters establish themselves immediately and "stay in the mind."

21 BRODIE, POLLY. "Fiction." *Library Journal* 105 (15 June):1410.
   Review of *A Glass of Blessings.* This understated tale about the search for happiness gives to the 1950s an ethos of "remote serenity."

22 BROWNE, JOSEPH. "Novels." *Philadelphia Inquirer,* 24 August, p. H13.
    Review of *A Glass of Blessings.* Refers to the novel's "agonizingly monotonous contents" and lack of passion.

23 BRUNSDALE, MITZI. "Pleasure from a Much Underrated British Author." *Houston Post,* 9 November, p. 53.
    Review of *A Few Green Leaves.* Finds parallels between Pym's writing and that of Dorothy Sayers, Josephine Tey, and P.D. James.

24 BRYFONSKI, DEDRIA, ed. "Pym, Barbara (Mary Crampton) 1913-." In *Contemporary Literary Criticism: Excerpts from Criticism of the Works of Today's Novelists, Poets, Playwrights, and Other Creative Writers,* Vol. 13. Detroit: Gale, pp. 469-71.
    Excerpted: 1977.27; 1978.25, 43, 48, 58.

25 BUCKMASTER, HENRIETTA. "High Comedy–Deftly Hidden." *Christian Science Monitor,* 12 May, p. B7.
    Review of *A Glass of Blessings.* Speculates that Pym was rediscovered because she addresses an "irresistible part of human life–high comedy." Pym observes her characters and their world without judgment. Her insights are "light and oblique but flashingly brilliant." Excerpted: 1981.17.

26 BUTCHER, MARYVONNE. "Ironies and Crises." *Tablet,* 16 August, p. 512.
    Brief review of *A Few Green Leaves.* Pym's "gentle and yet quite ruthless" observations of English village life make this an enjoyable book.

27 CLARK, ANNE. "Posthumous Disappointment from Pym." *Los Angeles Times Book Review,* 12 October, p. 13.
    Review of *A Few Green Leaves.* Owing to its absence of plot, a novel of this kind must depend heavily on characterization. "Here, unfortunately, Pym fails." She does not exploit fully the opportunities her heroine has for observing and analyzing human behavior. Instead, the novel is full of "haphazard glances."

28 CLEMONS, WALTER. "An Unnoticed World." *Newsweek* 95 (14 April):96, 99.
    Review of *A Glass of Blessings.* In this "magical" novel, "one of her best," Pym is able to enlist the reader's interest in a heroine "a

more ambitious novelist would either discard as not worth writing about or subject to satirical scorn."

29 COLE, THOMAS. "Barbara Pym's Last Novel: A Kind of Summing Up." *Baltimore Sun,* 21 September, p. 21.

Review of *A Few Green Leaves.* Calls this "a beautifully integrated and cleverly sustained low-keyed comedy." Praises her writing ("clear and simple"), her insights ("keen and unrelenting"), and her prejudices ("on the side of the angels"). Like Muriel Spark, her basic strength is her irony; unlike Spark, she grew stronger with each succeeding book.

30 COOK, BRUCE. "The Art of Making Routine Lives Absorbing." *Detroit News,* 21 September, p. E2.

Says that Pym is an overrated artist, and objects particularly to the comparisons made by reviewers and other critics between her and Jane Austen. Finds very little surface to her work at all and her characters often rather boring; yet it is Pym's "considerable art" that she draws us into her characters' world and manages finally to absorb us with their routine lives. Finds this to be especially true in *A Few Green Leaves.*

31 D[ONAVIN], D[ENISE] P. "Fiction." *Booklist* 77 (15 September):100.

Review of *A Few Green Leaves.* Notes Pym's "anthropological perspective" in this "piquant tableau."

32 FAGG, MARTIN. "Village Life." *Church Times* (London), 25 July, p. 4.

Review of *A Few Green Leaves.* Notes recurring references to the *Church Times* in Pym's novels. "[B]eneath the surface sparkle that makes [her] novels such delightful and easy 'reads', there lurks a pretty deep disenchantment with human character and aspiration." But the entertainment is "as piquant as ever."

33 FAIRBANKS, ELLEN. "The Luxury of Summer Reading." *Ms.* 9 (July):30 – 31.

Brief review of *A Glass of Blessings.* Refers to Pym's wit and attention to small details in this novel of manners, recalling the works of Jane Austen and Margaret Drabble.

34 FEINSTEIN, ELAINE. "Fiction." *Times* (London), 17 July, p. D11.

Review of *A Few Green Leaves*. The passions here of the old and lonely are small, mean, and nasty. Pym's gaze is "snide and beady"; her vision of humanity is sad.

35 FINLAYSON, IAIN. "An Interview with Barbara Pym." *Literary Review*, no. 10, 23 February, pp. 2-5.

Pym answers questions about the novel as an art form, other writers, Cyril Connolly's *Enemies of Promise*, politics, distractions from her writing, London and Oxford, the Arts Council, television, and her experiences with publishers.

36 FITZGERALD, PENELOPE. "A Secret Richness." *London Review of Books*, 22 November, p. 19.

Review of *A Few Green Leaves*. Finds "pity for lost opportunities" and a courageous opening to the future in this "elegiac and hopeful" book. Although Pym's comedy is high comedy, the issues are not comic at all. Discusses texture, background, and three kinds of conflict that recur throughout her novels: growing old, holding on to some measure of individuality, and adjusting the "vexatious distance" between the sexes. Excerpted: 1981.17.

37 FULLER, EDMUND. "Finding a Lifetime Friend in a Writer's Work." *Wall Street Journal*, 20 October, p. 26.

Overview of Pym's life and career. "She is a joy." Comments on *A Glass of Blessings* ("quietly delightful"), *Excellent Women*, *The Sweet Dove Died* ("subtle study of possessiveness self-defeated"), *Quartet in Autumn* ("deftly compassionate, poignant comedy"), and *A Few Green Leaves*. Notes similarities to Jane Austen in discernment of characterization and acute observations, loyalty to enduring values, rich vein of wry humor, and compassion. "Both involve us deeply in the subtle dramas of quiet lives."

38 GILMAN, JAYNE. "The Private Life of an Oxfordshire Village." *Oxford Mail*, 24 July, p. 22.

Brief review of *A Few Green Leaves*. Admires Pym but finds it difficult warming up to her in this "ruefully ironic, delicately witty" picture of a typical English village.

39 GOLD, EDITH. "A Talented Writer's Last Book." *Miami Herald*, 28 September, p. E6.

Review of *A Few Green Leaves*. Finds this to be both "stirring and enormously funny" because of Pym's "subtle wit and extraordinary psychological insight."

40 GORDON, CECELIA. "Indexers in Fiction." *Indexer* 12 (October):108-9.

Review of *No Fond Return of Love*. Pym is as "sweet and sour" as ever in this novel as she "gently denigrates and pokes fun" at her characters. Includes summary of her rediscovery. Recommends this book to indexers, "though they will find the portraits of themselves and their colleagues all too brief and tantalizing."

41 HARVEY, ELIZABETH. "A Last Novel." *Birmingham Post*, 20 November, p. 8.

Review of *A Few Green Leaves*. Pym's writing is sometimes as concentrated as poetry. Finds here no shadow of her own death but only a "deep serenity" in her story of village life.

42 HIGGENS, ALISON. "The Last Book by One of the Best." *Sacramento Bee*, 19 October, p. 33.

Review of *A Few Green Leaves*.

43 HILDEBRAND, HOLLY. "A Final Wonderful Novel from Barbara Pym." *St. Louis Globe-Democrat*, 11-12 October, p. 17.

Review of *A Few Green Leaves*. "Nobody can find the extraordinary in the ordinary in quite the same way and serve it up with such a poignant blend of laughter and tears as this witty British novelist." Finds here Pym's "special brand of magic" as she interweaves the lives of Emma and "a motley group of endearing characters."

44 H[OOPER], W[ILLIAM] B[RADLEY]. "Fiction." *Booklist* 76 (1 April):1109.

Review of *A Glass of Blessings*. This "wonderful novel" is reminiscent of Iris Murdoch and Margaret Drabble. The characters are well developed in "a splendid blend of humor and compassion ... written with deep empathy for human foibles."

45 KEMP, PETER. "Grave Comedy." *Listener* 104 (17 July):89.

Review of *A Few Green Leaves*. In this novel – "packed with calmly contemplated intimations of mortality" – Pym "ruefully sets the intellectual advantages of being an outsider against the emotional disadvantages." Notes Pym's attitudes to death ("cheerfully down-to-earth") and life ("slightly melancholy irony"). Excerpted: 1981.17.

46 KERSEY, ALAN. "Acid Humour from Angus." *Cambridge Evening News* (Cambridge), 31 July, p. 7.

Brief review of *A Few Green Leaves*. Sadly, this novel does nothing for Pym's reputation. The plot is a letdown after the "practically faultless" *The Sweet Dove Died.*

47 KING, FRANCIS. "Barbara Pym, a Lesson to Writers." *Sunday Telegraph* (London), 13 January, p. 19.

Obituary notice. From Pym's life novelists have learned that the "importance in ensuring their survival is neither transient fashions nor huge sales, but the admiration of a group, however small, of discriminating admirers." Within her self-imposed limits, she showed "unusual perception, grace and wit." Excerpted: 1981.17.

48 _____. "Fairly Excellent Woman." *Spectator* 245 (19 July):21-22.

Review of *A Few Green Leaves*. Finds it hard to substantiate current praise being accorded Pym and her novels. She was a good novelist, but not an outstanding one, as this novel makes clear: "beautifully shaped; every character is distinct; and there is not a page that is not irradiated with wit and fun." But her range is extremely narrow. "Not for her wuthering heights or lower depths, but merely the literary equivalent of the bland, cosy, comforting landscape of the Oxfordshire to which she retired." Pym knew her limitations and never attempted to exceed them. Excerpted: 1980.60.

49 K[IRK]-[GREENE], A[NTHONY] H.M. "Barbara Pym 1913-1980." *Africa* (London) 50 (January):94-95.

Reviews briefly Pym's life: her work at the International African Institute, her first six published novels, her rejection and subsequent rediscovery. Calls her a "modest, gentle and urbane colleague and friend."

50 KUBAL, DAVID. "Fiction Chronicle." *Hudson Review* 33 (Autumn):437-39.

Review of *A Glass of Blessings*. Notes Pym's perspective and tone and speculates why her novels are little read in America and why, after she had published six novels, she was rejected by her publisher. In this novel, Pym's view of society is "certainly outdated."

51 LEIGHTON, BETTY. "A Splendid New Beginning Is Aborted by Fate." *Winston-Salem* (N.C.) *Journal,* 26 October, p. 21.

Review of *A Few Green Leaves*. Finds brilliant Pym's "wry touch with social satire." She juxtaposes the banalities of modern life in the 1970s against historical time. "Demure tea parties, quiet walks through the woods, daily happenings are the perfect background for Pym's art."

The reader never misses more action. "She never labors a point." Pym stands alone among writers for what she has shown about "the sadnesses and comedies of everyday life."

52 LEVIN, BERNARD. "Fiction: Middle Marches. . . . ." *Sunday Times* (London), 27 July, p. 40.

Review of *A Few Green Leaves*. Calls this "thin, dull and very nearly pointless," in spite of Pym's fresh prose, knowledge of her characters, and control over the psychological and emotional believability of the story. "The real problem is that these characters cannot think of anything to do."

53 LIVELY, PENELOPE. "The World of Barbara Pym." *Literary Review* 79 (January):8-9.

There is a curious sense in which Pym seemed to spring to life fully fledged as a novelist, thirty years ago, and what has happened since has been not so much the process of learning by mistakes as a deliberate reworking and extension of an already mastered formula. In all of her novels, she is concerned with the perennial problems of being man or woman, old or young, vulnerable or impervious. *A Few Green Leaves,* for example, gives us a society complete in itself, constructed and peopled with all of Pym's artistry: believable, moving, entertaining. Reprinted: 1987.25.

54 McLEOD, KIRSTY. "A Few Green Leaves." *Country Life,* 25 September, p. 8.

Review of *A Few Green Leaves*. Praises Pym's exact eye for details, her wit, and her common sense, and notes parallels with Jane Austen.

55 MASSIE, ALLAN. "To Be Read with Muffins." *Scotsman* (Edinburgh), 2 August, p. 1.

Review of *A Few Green Leaves*. Finds this inferior to *The Sweet Dove Died,* "slow and slight," and likely to make readers wonder about the reasons behind Pym's revival. The characters are "very nice and very dull"; the prose is "self-conscious, whimsical, coy," far removed from the precision of Jane Austen. Suggests that Pym's writing is closer to that of Angela Thirkell.

56 MURPHY, MARESE. "Women Only?" *Irish Times,* 19 July, p. 8.

Review of *A Few Green Leaves*. Pym's "meticulous eye for social nuance" equipped her well to observe and chronicle events in the archetypal English village. Although the plot is of little consequence, it is "eminently readable."

57 NELSON, PATRICIA A. "Book Reviews." *Century: A Southwest Journal of Observation and Opinion,* 5 November, pp. 24-25.
General overview of the novels on the occasion of paperback editions. Comments on characters ("rather prim" but bold to choose a life alone), faith (habitual, but "unadorned by personal revelation"), and social class ("gradually more embattled"). "The ordinary struggle to live a life of grace is the obstinate nub of Pym's fiction." Finds in *Quartet in Autumn* "the clearest expression of Pym's wise and deliberate observation."

58 O. R. "Novels." *Daily Mail* (London), 10 July, p. 11.
Review of *A Few Green Leaves.* Calls this "a moving and humourously understated swan song" to the small-scale rural parishes Pym inhabited and loved. She was a "mistress of nostalgia [who] maps a cosy world we all hanker after."

59 OATES, JOYCE CAROL. "Books." *Mademoiselle* 86 (September):62-63.
Review of *A Glass of Blessings.* Calls her novels "beautifully orchestrated comedies of manners in which pretensions and absurd daydreams are deflated in witty, succinct, set-pieces." Likes particularly Pym's "unsentimental patience" with her characters.

60 OATES, QUENTIN. "Critics Corner." *Bookseller,* 26 July, 416-17.
Reviews critical reactions to *A Few Green Leaves.* Includes excerpts from 1980.14, 18, 48, 78.

61 OVERMYER, JANET. "Pym Novel Will Delight." *Columbus Dispatch* 22 June, p. J8.
Review of *A Glass of Blessings.* Calls this a revelation that is "more fascinating and believable than the hijinks in any number of splashier novels."

62 PINKHAM, PENNY. "Pym's Cup Full." *Boston Sunday Globe,* 11 May, pp. A8, 10.
Review of *A Glass of Blessings.* Praises this "elegant, chapter by chapter tease" for the author's sense of the ridiculous, deadpan delivery, eye for the unobtrusive and key details, presentation of character, and unforced style. She keeps the reader in doubt about her characters.

63 POOL, GAIL. "Doses of Reality." *New Boston Review* 5 (June/July):15-16.

Reviews Pym's first seven novels. *Excellent Women* epitomizes Pym's style, tone, and mode of writing. "Here there is no great drama, no sweeping gestures, no large motion; drama would be fictional, while Pym's own fiction strives for the ordinary which is *real.*" At the heart of her novels is the loss of "a framework, a structure for life, such as religion, or marriage, once provided." Given that, each character is haunted by the problem of finding a purpose in life.

64 RUBIN, MERLE. "The Real Miss Pym Is in Her Novels, Not Her Private Jottings." *Christian Science Monitor,* 23 August, p. 21.

Review of *A Very Private Eye.* Pym wrote the "quintessential novel." Her "instinctive wisdom" helped her to choose subjects that "by their very limitations gave her talents their greatest scope." The real Pym is not to be found in her diaries and journals, but in the fiction "she wove from life."

65 SCHMID, DOREEN. "Books." *Centervoice,* November, p. 27.

Review of *A Glass of Blessings.* Praises Pym for her clear voice that "gently and humorfully reveals the odd and subtle ties behind the scenes of the everyday." Notes similarities between Pym and Jane Austen and Anthony Powell.

66 SCHWARZBAUM, LISA. "A Cup of Pym." *Real Paper,* 14 June, p. 16.

"Pym's work is elegantly precise, wickedly observant, deceptively quiet, slyly funny, and beautifully written." Includes biographical background and praises *A Glass of Blessings.* "In minute, breathtaking ways, she sizes up the harms, the conventions, the pleasures, and the perversities of small lives and bestows upon them the rare beauty and clarity of her own genius."

67 SETON, CYNTHIA PROPPER. "Tea and Titillation in the Rectory." *Washington Post Book World,* 6 April, p. 5.

Review of *A Glass of Blessings.* This book – characterized by understatement, gentle irony, and precise choice of words – is a pleasure to dip into in peace and quiet. Pym celebrates the traditional values of responsibility, self-discipline, and discretion. Excerpted: 1981.17.

68 SEYMOUR-SMITH, MARTIN, ed. *Novels and Novelists: A Guide to the World of Fiction.* New York: St. Martin's, p. 203.

Brief overview of Pym's career and a discussion of her first ten novels.

69 SHRIMPTON, NICHOLAS. "Bucolic Bones." *New Statesman* 100 (15 August):17.

Review of *A Few Green Leaves.* Calls Pym a twentieth-century "minimalist." Her plot is "pared to the bone" and her technique is "peculiarly neutral." The result, paradoxically, is "a vivid sense of how we live now. . . . Beneath her inconsequential surface detail, in fact, Barbara Pym is here offering an artistic apologia."

70 SLUNG, MICHAEL. "Pym's Last Cup." *Washington Post Book World,* 12 October, p. 6.

Review of *A Few Green Leaves.* Pym's novels fall within the tradition of fiction concerned with "behaving properly." Wishes that this novel had "more of the sparkle" of the first books, but at the same time knows Pym's answer to that – " 'a small useless longing' " she would call it. Comments also on *Quartet in Autumn* ("unexpectedly downbeat") and *Excellent Women.*

71 SNOW, LOTUS. "The Trivial Round, the Common Task: Barbara Pym's Novels." *Research Studies* 48 (June):83-93.

In *Some Tame Gazelle* through *The Sweet Dove Died,* Pym – "a specialist in loneliness" – "scrupulously notes and records the behavior of 'ordinary people, people who have no claim to fame whatsoever'." In her first six novels, she holds her characters at a distance but treats them with "warm compassion" and gentle irony. With *Quartet in Autumn,* her observations of loneliness and rejection are made with "bleak detachment." In *The Sweet Dove Died* – "her most sophisticated and hollow novel" – Pym's detachment is particularly striking in her observations of people's behavior in "a contemporary world which recognizes no value but self-gratification." Reprinted: 1987.46.

72 STEWART, IAN. "Recent Fiction." *Illustrated London News* 268 (October):99.

Review of *A Few Green Leaves.* The narrative's "slender framework" shows the promise of "substantial development." But Pym's reputation as "a delicate, ironic miniaturist with a sympathetic insight into the comedy and pathos of the lives of unremarkable people" is due largely to *Quartet in Autumn* and *The Sweet Dove Died.*

73 THORNTON, JOHN. "Not So Small Change of Village Life." *Glasgow Herald,* 23 August, p. 8.

Review of *A Few Green Leaves*. Finds it difficult to convey the richness of Pym's work for those who are unfamiliar with it. In relating many chance meetings, dinners, coffee mornings, and social events, Pym "gives due weight to what was left unsaid and undone" and shows a sensitivity that invites comparisons with Jane Austen.

74 TREASE, GEOFFREY. "English Fiction." *British Book News,* December, p. 761.

Review of *A Few Green Leaves*. This is authentic Pym country, with its perceptive character observations, ironical humor, and subtle dialogue. "It is as though [Pym] had forgotten the bitterness of the wilderness, begun to enjoy her belated recognition, and . . . worked on with new confidence and zest."

75 TUCK, SHERRIE. "Fiction." *Library Journal* 105 (1 October):2108.

Brief review of *A Few Green Leaves*. Finds here the expected "literary skill and touching insight," the "gently wry humor and penetrating comments on modern life." Pym reflects thoughtfully on the role of the novelist in society and offers "a poignant meditation on the pilgrimage of life viewed in light of its destination, death."

76 WAUGH, AUBERON. "Out to Grass with Emma." *Standard* (London), 29 July, p. 13.

Review of *A Few Green Leaves*. Calls this "all quite painfully like real life." Probably Pym never intended her village as a microcosm of Britain in its postindustrial decline, but it does serve as a model. "A general air of absurdity attaches to everything which happens in this self-consciously crotchety society."

77 WHITE, EDWARD M. "Pym's Newest Cup and an American Marriage." *Los Angeles Times Book Review,* 8 June, p. 12.

Review of *A Glass of Blessings*. Pym's tough mind and gracious irony gives the reader a book that promises repeated pleasure with repeated readings. . . . The events are small but radiate meaning."

78 WILSON, A.N. "Thinking of Being Them." *Times Literary Supplement,* 18 July, p. 799.

Review of *A Few Green Leaves*. Calls Pym "the chronicler of quiet lives"; her characters are "as real and as rounded" as some of the best nineteenth-century fictional characters. Notes the sharp poignancy and loneliness of her characters in *Quartet in Autumn* and *The Sweet Dove Died* and the "hilarity" of *Some Tame Gazelle*. In *A Few Green Leaves,* Pym's "realism is sharper, the underlying poignancy more carefully implied," giving the reader the best of both "the early and the late Pym manner." Excerpted: 1980.60; 1981.17.

79 WRIGHT, HELEN. "Fiction." *Best Sellers* 40 (December):314-15.
Review of *A Few Green Leaves*. The townspeople give this novel "its strength and form." Calls it a "witty, graceful" book with "clean and crisp" writing and "alive" characters. Pym is a "delightful surprise."

1981

1 ALLEN, BRUCE. "Browsing." *Chicago Tribune Book World,* 14 June, p. 5.
Brief review of *Less Than Angels*. Calls this one of Pym's "sleekest and funniest novels." Praises her use of the "gossipy omniscient narrative voice," the comic professional rhetoric, and the dramatic irony. Pym's comedies of manners define their genre precisely.

2 ANON. "Briefly Noted: Fiction." *New Yorker* 57 (2 November):188.
Review of *Jane and Prudence*. In this very funny novel, Pym gives to her heroine Jane a sense of humor. Finds here many "comic complications."

3 ANON. "Fiction." *Booklist* 77 (1 January):615.
Review of *Less Than Angels*. Although this isn't Pym's best novel, it will be warmly received. Refers to her shrewd satire, intricate plot, and ordinary characters. The novel has a "continued freshness."

4 ANON. "Narrow Compass." *New Directions for Women* 10 (March/April):13.
Review of *Excellent Women, The Sweet Dove Died,* and *Quartet in Autumn*. Comments on the effects of any intrusion into the "small, contained" world in each of these novels. Reading them "brings back characters and personalities we have known, and who have known us."

5 ANON. "New Novels." *Spectator* 247 (5 December):23.
Brief review of *A Few Green Leaves*.

6 ANON. "Notes on Current Books: Fiction." *Virginia Quarterly Review* 57 (Spring):59-60.

Brief review of *A Few Green Leaves*. Mentions Pym's "quiet, unhurried style."

7 ANON. "PW Forecasts: Fiction." *Publishers Weekly* 220 (11 September):59.

Review of *Jane and Prudence*. This "gentle, folksy story" lacks "vigorous" characters or a "lively" plot, but "we can be amused by the quaint, unliberated ideas of Pym's women about themselves and the menfolk they rather patronizingly try to manage."

8 ANON. "Recommended Fiction." *Antioch Review* 39 (Fall):519.

Brief mention of *Less Than Angels*. "It's easy to become a fan, for her affectionate but wry humor is an import from England, of which there is always a short supply. Academics, particularly if fledgling anthropologists, are in this example forewarned."

9 AUCHINCLOSS, EVE. "Surprises of Comedy and Sadness." *New York Times Book Review*, 1 February, pp. 9, 25-26.

Review of *A Few Green Leaves*. Nothing much happens in Pym's novels. She remains "a skeptical, almost aloof, observer studying relationships with a discrimination that her anthropologists might envy." Being alone in this novel or in *Less Than Angels* "calls for dignity, patience, intellectual curiosity, and a sense of humor." Only superficialities separate these two books, but a talent for "enduring details" roots her novels "in life and gives them their momentum." Concludes that Pym finds both comedy and sadness in "the most banal and cozy moments without ever managing to be dull."

10 BRODIE, POLLY. "Fiction." *Library Journal* 106 (1 November):2154.

Brief review of *Jane and Prudence*. This understated tale – one of Pym's "most delightful" – will charm and amuse readers.

11 C., J. "Book Reviews." *Los Angeles Federal Savings Quarterly*, Summer, p. 34.

Brief review of *Less Than Angels*. Calls this "a wry story of contrasts" that will please all readers of Pym. Includes excerpt from 1981.15.

12 CROSLAND, MARGARET. *Beyond the Lighthouse: English Women Novelists in the Twentieth Century*. London: Constable, pp. 183-85.

Seeks to find if Pym has a philosophy and if her fascination with the Church would "put off" the secular reader. In *Quartet in Autumn,* finds "no bitterness, and a mature, serious attitude." *Some Tame Gazelle* is "an infinitely consoling work." Concludes that there is in her novels "an inherited spirit of goodness" without an attempt to propagate the gospel.

13 D[ONAVIN], D[ENISE] P. "Fiction." *Booklist* 78 (1 October):179.
Brief review of *Jane and Prudence.* "Pym's appealing characters carry the modest plot beautifully, with charm and wit. Excerpted: 1986.43.

14 DYER, RICHARD. "The Violence Runs beneath Surface." *Boston Globe,* 27 October, p. 16.
Review of *Jane and Prudence.* Calls Pym an important and very funny novelist "who used the techniques and subjects of the novel of manners for her own darker purposes." This novel is "a more purely comic invention [but] a less certain performance" than her later ones.

15 FULLER, EDMUND. "Stylish High Comedy and Astute Perception." *Wall Street Journal,* 2 March, p. 16.
Review of *Less Than Angels.* Notes the anthropological background to this novel and Pym's close observations of the comic both in the "private and professional behavior of her people." Like her other books, this one will reward both her established fans and new readers. Excerpted: 1981.11.

16 GIBBONS, JAMES. "Pym: A Magellan of the Everyday." *Houston Chronicle,* 20 December, p. 21.
Review of *Jane and Prudence.* All of Pym's characters are well drawn in a novel that marks her achievement as a sociologist and her triumph as a writer. Praises Pym's ability to show the "drama of daily life and 'ordinary' people."

17 GUNTON, SHARON R., ed. "Pym, Barbara 1913-1980." In *Contemporary Literary Criticism: Excerpts from Criticisms of the Works of Today's Novelists, Poets, Playwrights, Short Story Writers, Filmmakers, Screenwriters, and Other Creative Writers.* Vol. 19. Detroit: Gale, pp. 386-89.
Includes excerpts from 1977.20; 1978.19; 1980.25, 36, 45, 47, 67, 78.

18 HARVEY, STEPHEN. "Brief Encounters." *Village Voice,* 2 December, p. 56.

Review of *Jane and Prudence.* Finds parallels between Pym's novels and those of Angela Thirkell, E.F. Benson, and Jane Austen. "Her style is so terse and controlled as to seem utterly effortless – and beneath all that gentility lurks a savagely comic vision." Like *Excellent Women,* this novel is "a common-sense tribute to the spirit of making do with life's dim compromises, and extracting a kind of triumph from them." Finds her observations of "homely human detail . . . as potent as ever."

19 H[OOPER], W[ILLIAM] B[RADLEY]. "Fiction." *Booklist* 77 (1 January):615.

Brief review of *Less Than Angels.* "Not Pym's best, the novel is certainly not plain, either." Notes the shrewd satire, intricate plot, and characters that are attractive in their ordinariness. The novel's "continued freshness is to be marveled at." Excerpted: 1986.43.

20 KENNEDY, JOSEPH PATRICK. "Pym: Studying the Anthropologists." *Houston Chronicle-Sun,* 25 January, p. 33.

Brief review of *Less Than Angels.* "Miss Pym develops her story with a precision that compensates for the novel's occasional slow passages by its subtle dialogue, numerous cups of tea, gin, professional professors, and men and women who are less than angels."

21 KESSLER, JULIA BRAUN. "Reprinting Pym's Prim and Not-So-Proper Characters." *Los Angeles Times Book Review,* 24 May, p. 10.

Review of *Less Than Angels.* Calls Pym "not just a skilled stylist and a sprightly wit but the creator of a world as compelling as it is complete." Is rather skeptical of comparing Pym to Jane Austen, though there are resemblances in their "intensely regional and remarkably timeless" characters, their sensibilities, and their humor.

22 KING, NINA. "Barbara Pym: Middle-Class Wry." *Newsday,* 8 February, pp. 20-21.

Review of *Less Than Angels* and *A Few Green Leaves.* Like Jane Austen, Pym is a "meticulous worker in miniature." Their observations of "individual foibles and patterns of social absurdity" are witty and sharp-eyed. They share an implicit sense of people's limitations. Although both are concerned with suitable behavior, Pym "writes in an age when the suitable is no longer self-evident."

23 KUBAL, DAVID. "Fiction Chronicle." *Hudson Review* 34 (Autumn):462-63.

Review of *Less Than Angels*. Praises it as possibly her best novel. Certainly it is "more richly humorous and generous" than those she wrote immediately before her death. "Hers is a world of repression, which both pains the self and permits it to survive, relatively secure from the forces that would absorb it." Excerpted: 1986.43.

24 LEIGHTON, BETTY. "Pym Explores Foibles and Vanities of Us All." *Winston-Salem* (N.C.) *Journal,* 15 February, p. 17.

Review of *Less Than Angels*. Comments on the self-deluded characters, leisurely pace, and tongue-in-cheek humor. Pym's comic novels are "informed by a subtle intelligence that is serious, germane, and more than anything else, healthy." The heroine, Catherine Oliphant, strikes a balance between "the needs of pleasure and of autonomy."

25 LOCHER, FRANCES C., ed. "Pym, Barbara (Mary Crampton) 1913-1980." In *Contemporary Authors: A Bio-Bibliographical Guide to Current Writers in Fiction, General Nonfiction, Poetry, Journalism, Drama, Motion Pictures, Television, and Other Fields*. Vols. 97-100. Detroit: Gale, p. 449.

Brief Obituary.

26 LODICO, MICHAEL. "Quiet Yet Powerful Barbara Pym." *Greensboro* (N.C.) *Daily News Record,* 17 May, p. 13.

Review of *A Few Green Leaves*. In contemporary fiction Pym's novels are "outstanding . . . for the wit, compassion and subtle moral discrimination [she] employs in chronicling unremarkable lives." But finds here a less lighthearted atmosphere. Of Pym's heroines, Emma is both the weakest and the dullest, never seeming to come to life. "What redeems the novel are the minor characters and Pym's portrayal of [the most memorable character in the novel] a late twentieth-century village haunted by its own history."

27 McALLER, JOHN. "Fiction." *Best Sellers* 40 (March):428.

Review of *Less Than Angels*. Finds parallels between Pym's satire and that of Evelyn Waugh's, "laced with vitriol." But this novel is "rollicking fun." Her heroines are not Miss Marples, but "wistful, unfulfilled women, the odd bits left in the tiderack by the retreating ocean of empire." Excerpted: 1986.43.

28 OVERMYER, JANET. "Recent and Readable." *Columbus Dispatch,*
15 March, p. 12.
    Review of *Less Than Angels.* This novel confirms Pym's ability
"to draw exquisite sketches of people and situations which imply
considerable depth." She views her characters as might an
anthropologist, "with wry, clear-sighted affection."

29 PHILLIPS, ROBERT. "Narrow, Splendid Work." *Commonweal* 108
(8 May):284-85.
    Review of *A Few Green Leaves.* Pym's writing is "dense with
psychological insight and larded with wit." Praises the characterization
in this ambitious novel as "fully-drawn" and its feelings as "highly
palpable." Because she pits the present against the past and parades
history before the reader "in the living flesh," Pym's final novel
approaches the "daring and conceit" of Virginia Woolf's *Between the
Acts.*

30 SEYMOUR-SMITH, MARTIN. "The British Novel 1976-1980."
British Book News, June, p. 325.
    Calls Pym "an exquisite minor" novelist. *Quartet in Autumn* is
"less wide in scope" than *The Sweet Dove Died,* which he calls "a
psychologically impeccable and subtle record of a nasty but courageous
woman's battle against self-rejection."

31 SILVER, ADELE Z. "Modest but Witty World of Barbara Pym."
Cleveland Plain Dealer, 7 June 1981, p. 21.
    Review of *Less Than Angels.* Notes the differences between
Pym's novels and those by Margaret Drabble and Doris Lessing. The
world of this novel, like all of her work, is a quiet world, yet "so rich
with insight, wit, and style."

32 STROUSE, JEAN. "Elegant Surgery." *Newsweek* 97 (19 January):84.
    Review of *Less Than Angels.* Echoes of Jane Austen and
Charlotte Brontë in Pym's voice are "stronger than ever" in this novel.
Like the best writers of romantic fiction, Pym is "human and funny and
sad."

33 ZUCKERMAN, AMY. "Making the Ordinary Fascinating." *Worcester*
(Mass.) *Sunday Telegraph,* 1 March, p. 17.
    Review of *Less Than Angels.* Pym's style is "distinctly" twentieth
century and post-Freudian. Finds that unlike the other novels, here the
emphasis is on the satire rather than on the characters. But like the

other works, this novel offers "a fascinating peek into another world." Pym has that rare talent of "making the ordinary fascinating."

1982

1 ACKROYD, PETER. "Survival of the Faithful." *Sunday Times* (London), 21 February, p. 43.

Review of *An Unsuitable Attachment.* Finds here "great richness of theme and language combined with a certain hesitancy." The story's telling is neither trite nor familiar. Because Pym stays so close to her characters, "she can invest such life with an imaginative sympathy and depth which precludes any easy irony–or scorn." Disagrees with Larkin's reference to the book's "undiminished high spirits" (*see* 1982.39). Although the characters are church-going, they have "precious little faith." Finds here "a troubled vision . . . which underlies its comic or realistic detail." Calls it a "vision of emptiness." Excerpted: 1982.49.

2 ALABASTER, CAROL. " 'Twentieth Century Jane Austen' Sheds Light on England." *Arizona Republic,* 25 July, p. 13.

Brief review of *An Unsuitable Attachment.* Considers parallels with Jane Austen's novels while looking at Pym's irony, humor, and characterization.

3 A[LLEN], B[RUCE]. "New Fiction and Nonfiction: Briefly Noted." *Christian Science Monitor,* 7 July, p. 17.

Brief review of *An Unsuitable Attachment.* Calls Pym a minor artist whose "books retain their essential effervescence and charm." Her latest is another "imperturbably droll comedy of romantic manners."

4 _____. "Summer's Buried treasures: 'The Winter People' and Other Neglected Fiction." *Chicago Tribune Book World,* 1 August, p. 1.

Brief review of *An Unsuitable Attachment.* Finds in Pym's novels "real literary substance [as] brilliant adaptions of the method and manner of Jane Austen." This one is a "delightfully accomplished comedy, rife with wry dialogue and nicely absurd names . . . and brightened immeasurably by the curmudgeonly personality of a cat called Faustina."

5 ANON. "Briefly Noted: Fiction." *New Yorker* 58 (24 May):133-34.

Review of *An Unsuitable Attachment.* Finds it difficult to understand why Pym's publishers rejected this novel. The cat in the novel seems at times to be Pym's alter ego: "sly, cool, and equipped with retractable claws."

6 ANON. "Fiction." *Kirkus Reviews* 50 (15 March):367.
    Review of *An Unsuitable Attachment.* "Pym seems more drawn to pathos than to comedy here, but she's not yet ready . . . to give up happy endings for ironic bleakness." The characters' transformations are unconvincing. "And throughout, one has the sense of an instinct for the sad, cruel truth that's been reined-in and smoothed over." Praises those "marvelous moments" when library and religious matters arise.

7 ANON. "Fiction." *Kirkus Reviews* 50 (1 November):1216.
    Brief review of *No Fond Return of Love.* This "gently comic" novel is a welcome addition, featuring "mildly amorous professors and quietly yearning spinsters headed for a shaky but happy ending."

8 ANON. "PW Forecasts: Fiction." *Publishers Weekly* 221 (2 April):69.
    Review of *An Unsuitable Attachment.* Calls this one of Pym's best because of its decorous, gentle humor, its leisurely unfolding of the narrative, and its wonderful cameo portraits.

9 ANON. "PW Forecasts: Fiction." *Publishers Weekly* 222 (15 October):47.
    Review of *No Fond Return of Love.* Dulcie Mainwaring's character comes to life in this latest comedy of manners. Pym could be the twentieth century's answer to Jane Austen.

10 BARGREEN, MELINDA. "Pym Deftly Captures Human Foibles and Follies." *Seattle Times,* 21 February, p. 23.
    Review of *Jane and Prudence.* Praises this as a "witty and trenchant account of life in an English village, . . . written with a mature eye to human foibles and follies."

11 BECKER, ALIDA. " 'Lost' Novel Well Worth Discovering." *Philadelphia Inquirer,* 1 August, p. 6.
    Review of *An Unsuitable Attachment.* Calls this a "deceptively modest," quiet glimpse at a group of quiet lives; it reveals much more about human nature than many books with "loftier pretensions."

12 B[ELL], H[AZEL] K. "Indexers in Fiction." *Indexer* 13 (April):26.
    Offers thirteen quotations from *No Fond Return of Love* in which indexing and romance are intertwined.

13 BROTHERS, BARBARA. "Women Victimised by Fiction: Living and Loving in the Novels by Barbara Pym." In *Twentieth-Century Women Novelists.* Edited by Thomas F. Staley. London: Macmillan; Totowa, N.J.: Barnes & Noble, pp. 61-80.

Examines the challenge to the romantic paradigm that echoes in all of Pym's novels. "Though her portrayal of life focuses on its mundaneness and on her characters' self-deceptions and self-pretensions, Pym's is not the pen of a satirist." Her characters seem remote from the modern world, their prospects are dim, but revealed is Pym's sensibility and her deep understanding of human nature. Excerpted: 1986.43.

14 BROYARD, ANATOLE. "Overflowing Her Situation." *New York Times Book Review,* 15 August, p. 27.

Finds Pym's "most brilliant achievement" to be the portrait of the archetypal "Woman Who Overflows Her Situation." Jane of *Jane and Prudence* is the best example with its recognizable theme of "the runaway growth of women and the comparative diminishment of men." Pym's irony is "specially fitted; it is exactly Jane's shape and nobody else's." Excerpted: 1986.43.

15 BUTCHER, MARYVONNE. "Period Piece." *Tablet,* 13 March, p. 22.

Review of *An Unsuitable Attachment.* "This novel, though tightly constructed, alive with interesting people and written with malicious humour, is still an anachronism: we can read it now as a period piece of real quality."

16 BUTLER, MARILYN. "Keeping Up with Jane Austen." *London Review of Books,* 6 May, pp. 16-17.

Review of *An Unsuitable Attachment.* Finds "verbal and explicit" debts to Jane Austen, particularly in the characters. In Pym's world, the characters and institutions are "strangely and bleakly" transformed. Excerpted: 1986.43.

17 C., J.C. "Fiction." *Los Angeles Federal Savings Quarterly,* Spring, pp. 31, 34.

Review of *Jane and Prudence.* Calls Prudence "beautiful, elegant, meticulous, endlessly involved in discreet, hopeless romantic affairs." Jane, on the other hand, is "decidedly 'frumpy'," absentminded, and discomforting to others.

18 CALISHER, HORTENSE. "Enclosures: Barbara Pym." *New Criterion* 1 (September):53-56.

Discusses the kinds of books that are antecedents of Pym – those offering a "comfortingly localized place and domestic character." Considers *Excellent Women, Less Than Angels, A Glass of Blessings, The Sweet Dove Died, A Few Green Leaves,* and *An Unsuitable Attachment.* "What one asks of the great enclosures (and gets) is an assurance that the sequestration is natural within the life of the times, and within human nature as well."

19 CAMPBELL, JAMES. "Kitchen Window." *New Statesman* 103 (19 February):25.

Review of *An Unsuitable Attachment.* Finds in the first fifty pages a sure "gently satirical touch," after which Pym seems unsure of what to do with her characters. Too many of them have approximately equal weight here. Is not surprised that her publishers rejected it. Excerpted: 1986.43.

20 CANTWELL, MARY. "Books of the Times." *New York Times,* 10 May, p. 21.

Review of *An Unsuitable Attachment.* Considers Pym as a descendant of Jane Austen. "What Miss Pym is writing about, in her amused, astringent manner, is the human need to be linked." She does this without ever raising her voice.

21 CARLO, MICHAEL. "Fiction." *Best Sellers* 42 (August):175.

Brief review of *An Unsuitable Attachment.* Calls this "an anachronism," hardly relevant to our times, but "a pleasant diversion."

22 CHAPMAN, DEIRDRE. "Lost Horizons in North London." *Glasgow Herald,* 20 February, p. 11.

Review of *An Unsuitable Attachment.* Considers the novel's weakness (the author seems to be "locked in" with her characters) and strength (the "authentic graveness and whimsy" of the middle class). Calls the novel "shrunk."

23 CULLINAN, ELIZABETH. "Books: Critics' Christmas Choices." *Commonweal* 109 (3 December):658-59.

Recommends *An Unsuitable Attachment* as a book in which the writer revels "in details of English character and custom, bares the state of perpetually conflicting emotions out of which we all speak and even act."

24 CUNNINGHAM, VALENTINE. "A World of Ordinary Gentlefolk." *Observer* (London), 21 February, p. 32.

Review of *An Unsuitable Attachment.* "[T]his novel makes the oddities of its snobbish, catty, parson-respecting tribe precisely the object of its waspish attentions." Notes that Pym's "wry warmth" is combined with a "continual sense of impending horror." Perhaps this helps to explain why the novel was rejected in 1963.

25 DANIEL, MARGARET. "Period Piece." *Church Times* (London), 19 February, p. 5.

Review of *An Unsuitable Attachment.* Pym uses her original talent to offer "a period piece of considerable charm." Although its development is somewhat thin, admirers will enjoy those "perceptive, funny, dexterous ways that give her writing its distinctive quality."

26 DAVIES, DAVID TWISTON. "Recent Fiction." *Daily Telegraph* (London), 18 February, p. 13.

Review of *An Unsuitable Attachment.* In spite of the plot's "indulgent air" and the unprepared-for happy ending, "with its self-consciously Jane Austen values the story is shrewdly told and has great charm." Considers the reasons her publishers rejected it. Excerpted: 1982.49.

27 DONAHUE, DEIRDRE. "The Lost Novel of a Latter-Day Jane Austen." *Washington Post Book World,* 20 June, p. 6.

Review of *An Unsuitable Attachment.* Calls this "vintage Pym," equal to her previous novels. "The publisher must have been mad to reject this jewel. The cut-glass elegance of her precise, understated wit sparkles; her understanding of the human heart gleams more softly but just as bright." Notes her gift for the "telling phrase," her deep interest in religion, and her handling of class and sexual differences and the barriers to love they often erect.

28 D[ONAVIN], D[ENISE] P. "Fiction." *Booklist* 78 (15 April):1042.

Brief review of *An Unsuitable Attachment.* Not Pym's best – it suffers from "excessive wordiness" – but this novel is "still an engaging work of fiction."

29 DUCHÊNE, ANNE. "Handing on Loneliness." *Times Literary Supplement,* 26 February, p. 214.

Review of *An Unsuitable Attachment.* Responds to Larkin's commentary on the novel (*see* 1982.39) and considers why it was rejected by her publisher. This is not "vintage Pym." Missing, for example, are the "delicate desperations" that warmed *Excellent Women.* But Pym's fifteen years' suspension as a published writer must have led to a "withdrawal of confidence" and a loss of "many more pleasures than the book itself happens to provide."

30 DYER, RICHARD. "Rediscovering Barbara Pym." *Boston Globe,* 25 May, p. 21.

Review of *An Unsuitable Attachment.* Notes that Pym uses the techniques of the comic social novelist "to depict a particularly bleak view of life." Finds here the "unmistakable and indispensable" voice of Pym.

31 _____. "The Sharply Observant Barbara Pym." *Boston Globe,* 21 December, p. 34.

Review of *No Fond Return of Love.* "No contemporary novelist has been more comprehensively observant about the things she knew, and therefore about everything else." Calls this a "deftly plotted, tender, and hilarious novel," recommended to anyone who has felt loneliness and needs to laugh about it.

32 ELLIOTT, JANICE. "Thunder of Teacups." *Sunday Telegraph* (London), 21 February, p. 22.

Review of *An Unsuitable Attachment.* Once the reader has stepped into Pym's world, it is hard to leave. The feeling of "something feral, fierce and not very nice just below the surface" gives this work its edge. Excerpted: 1982.49.

33 FULLER, EDMUND. "An Anthropologist of the English Middle Class." *Wall Street Journal,* 25 May, p. 30.

Review of *Jane and Prudence* and *An Unsuitable Attachment.* Comments on the gentle ironic detachment in the former; Pym perceives every "foible and eccentricity" of the Church of England. The latter is in her "best vein" and roves farther afield than the other novels. "Hers is essentially a kindly comic talent, occasionally, particularly in *Quartet in Autumn,* quietly rueful. It is in her comic spirit, deft style, and keenness of observation that she most seems like a Jane Austen of our time."

34 GOLD, EDITH. "Pym's Novel Finds Deserved Home." *Miami Herald,* 15 July, p. 22.

Review of *An Unsuitable Attachment.* Finds here "wonderful" characters and a plot that is "warm and funny, with as much bite" as any of Pym's other books.

35 GORDON, MARY. "Symposium: Books That Gave Me Pleasure."
New York Times Book Review, 5 December, p. 52.
Says she read *No Fond Return of Love* and *An Unsuitable Attachment* with "sheer joy." Grieves that there are no more new novels by Pym to turn to.

36 HARVEY, ELIZABETH. "Drama of the Commonplace."
Birmingham Post, 1 March, p. 15.
Review of *An Unsuitable Attachment.* This entertaining novel is in the "mood" of Pym's earlier books. Although the title misleads, the word "attachment" fits "comfortably" into the novel's pattern.

37 H[OOPER], W[ILLIAM] B[RADLEY]. "Fiction." *Booklist* 79 (1 December):484.
Brief review of *No Fond Return of Love.* Comments on Pym's satiric understatement, great understanding of and fondness for her characters, and "most satisfying" resolution.

38 KEMP, PETER. "Pym's No. 7." *Listener* 107 (18 February):24.
Review of *An Unsuitable Attachment.* "Occasionally anticipating the more powerful later books, this novel constantly recapitulates the earlier." Like that of its heroine, the "occasional hesitancy [in this novel] ... is the hesitation of transition, a not-quite-assured move towards something more demanding." Pym's talent matured after this novel, "into the posed, sharpened satire of *The Sweet Dove Died,* the elegiac bleakness of *Quartet in Autumn,* the open-eyed almost euphoric stoicism of *A Few Green Leaves.*" Her publishers were imperceptive not to have seen these qualities emerging here. Excerpted: 1982.49.

39 LARKIN, PHILIP. Foreword to *An Unsuitable Attachment.* London: Macmillan, pp. 5-10.
The rejection in 1963 of Pym's seventh novel *(An Unsuitable Attachment)* by the publisher under whose imprint her first six novels had appeared meant that she remained unpublished for the next fourteen years. Recounts his friendship with Pym during this notorious episode of postwar publishing history, giving the publisher's side as reported by the present head of the firm, Tom Maschler. Reprinted as "The Rejection of Barbara Pym": 1987.23; Responded to: 1982.1, 29, 42.

40 LEIGHTON, BETTY. "A Good Novel Was Rejected, a Career Blighted." *Winston-Salem* (N.C.) *Journal,* 30 May, p. C4.

Review of *An Unsuitable Attachment*. Considers possible reasons that this novel was originally rejected, then discusses it as an "excellent novel" that equals and in some way surpasses her previous books. "Barbara Pym had a keen eye and an unerring instinct for comedy, tragicomedy and plain ordinary everyday life."

41 LEVINE, SUZANNE. "The Luxury of Summer Reading." *Ms.* 10 (June):18.
    Brief review of *An Unsuitable Attachment*. Calls this "wonderful, vintage, bittersweet Pym, perhaps more sweet than bitter this time."

42 LIVELY, PENELOPE. "Recent Fiction." *Encounter* 58 (April):76-78.
    Review of *An Unsuitable Attachment*. "It is a wonderful book: hilarious, unexpected, touching and occasionally faintly disturbing." Disagrees with Larkin's criticisms of the narrative (*see* 1982.39). The "vaguely unspecified" unsuitability of the match between Ianthe Broome and John Challow seems characteristic of Pym's "indeterminate unsettling situation." Finds it surprising that feminists have never claimed Pym, for no other woman novelist deals as effectively with "male aspirations." Excerpted: 1986.43.

43 McLEOD, KIRSTY. "Women of the Cloth." *Yorkshire Post,* 4 March, p. 17.
    Review of *An Unsuitable Attachment*. The following qualities in Pym's writing are "timeless" and "perfectly suited" to the world she portrays: "English understatedness, minute observation and a wry, occasionally deliciously catty sense of humour."

44 MARS-JONES, ADAM. "Pym's Number Two." *Financial Times* (London), 27 February, p. 27.
    Review of *An Unsuitable Attachment*. The possible unsuitability of Ianthe's attachment – "in a world without autocratic fathers and rigid taboos" – is dated and therefore unconvincing. Elsewhere, however, Pym's method is up to date by including an anthropologist, giving her "another set of standards by which to judge human behavior." Pym's style makes the novel "pleasurable and rewarding" to read.

45 MARSH, PAMELA. "Pym – Subtle and Accomplished." *Christian Science Monitor,* 29 December, p. 15.
    Review of *No Fond Return of Love*. Comments on Pym's reputation, characters ("middle-aged, educated gentlewomen with intellectual leanings, content to live alone, but not lonely"), and irony

behind a "conventional, often mousy, façade." Says these "packed pages are well worth lingering over."

46 MILLER, ROGER. "Underrated, Overrated, It's Pure Pym." *Milwaukee Journal,* 13 June, p. 27.
   Review of *An Unsuitable Attachment.* The novels by this exceptionally talented writer will stand the test of time. She shares with Jane Austen a "lively sense of fun," but lacks the same degree of irony. Notes parallels between Pym and E.F. Benson and Angela Thirkell.

47 MILTON, EDITH. "Worlds in Miniature." *New York Times Book Review,* 20 June, p. 11.
   Review of *An Unsuitable Attachment.* The lives of Pym's characters "commemorate the death of a civilization," the "bygone mysteries of the Church of England and the lost snobberies of empire." Finds it incredible that the novel was rejected by her publisher. Calls it "a paragon of a novel, certainly one of her best, witty, elegant." Excerpted: 1986.43.

48 MONTEITH, CHARLES. "Publishing Larkin." *Times Literary Supplement,* 21 May, p. 552.
   Quotes from a letter written by Larkin to Faber & Faber regarding the rejection of *An Unsuitable Attachment.*

49 OATES, QUENTIN. "Critics Corner." *Bookseller,* 27 February, pp. 801-3.
   Reviews critical reactions to *An Unsuitable Attachment.* Includes excerpts of: 1982.1, 26, 32, 38, 57-58, 68.

50 OROWAN, FLORELLA. "Learned Men and Brussels Sprouts." *Fiction, Literature & the Arts Review* 13 (Autumn):45.
   Review of *No Fond Return of Love.* Calls this "a rather blatant parody" of Jane Austen's *Mansfield Park.* As in all of Pym's novels, a final saving grace rescues her characters from an "anti-heroic abyss."

51 OVERMYER, JANET. "Late Author's Tale Scores Anew." *Columbus Sunday Dispatch,* 12 July, p. H11.
   Review of *An Unsuitable Attachment.* Comments on Pym's "wit, precision of expression, intelligence, lovingly drawn characters, intertwined marriage plots, misunderstandings, common sense and lack of same." Finds the novel to be "somewhat darker" than her other works.

52 PHILLIPS, ROBERT. "Posthumous Pym." *Ontario Review* 32 (Fall/Winter):114-15.

Review of *An Unsuitable Attachment.* In some respects this is typical Pym, but not one of her finest. Notes similarities with Jane Austen in the "comic characterization, sense and sensibility, head and heart, rest and motion, wit and plain talk." And for the first time an animal, the Vicar's wife's cat, becomes an important character.

53 R., R. "In Print." *Inquiry* 24 (December):43.

Brief mention of *No Fond Return of Love.* "Profound in an unprepossessing way, the work is another of Pym's astringent seriocomedies about circumscribed female lives."

54 REDMOND, LUCILE. "Pym's Number 7." *Irish Times,* 6 March, p. 7.

Review of *An Unsuitable Attachment.* Calls this a "tired book, halting, proper, adverb-ridden, its humour ... dated and, worse, mistimed." Pym's style is "over-explanatory, the rhythm halts and hobbles, the words are chosen for ease before accuracy." Properly edited, this could have been a very funny book.

55 REEFER, MARY M. "A Tender Irony Enlightens Lives of Lonely Gentility." *Kansas City* (Mo.) *Star,* 13 June, pp. K1, 10.

Review of *An Unsuitable Attachment.* Discusses the characters' "low-keyed but insistent snobbery," powers of observation, good manners, employment, and interest in the opposite sex. Recommends the book to all readers of Pym.

56 ROWSE, A.L. "Books of the Year." *Spectator* 249 (18 December):45.

Cites *A Few Green Leaves* as "just my cup of (her favourite) Earl Grey."

57 SEYMOUR, MIRANDA. "Fiction." *Times* (London), 18 February, p. 10.

Review of *An Unsuitable Attachment.* Mentions Pym's plots ("slight, elegantly constructed"), wit ("always acute, never vicious"), and world ("small, but ... all her own and perfectly comprehended"). Is less pleased with her frequent authorial interjections of a "mildly homiletic nature." Pym's domain lies somewhere between Trollope's Barset and E.F. Benson's "maliciously be-spinstered Rye." Excerpted: 1982.49.

58 SHRAPNEL, NORMAN. "Pym's Number Two." *Guardian* (Manchester), 18 February, p. 14.

Review of *An Unsuitable Attachment*. Finds here "a kind of social shiftiness," a "chaste, chilly world" in which all men are brothers. The title is misleading. Although characteristic of Pym and therefore enjoyable to read, it is "nowhere near her best work." Excerpted: 1982.49.

59 SILVER, ADELE Z. "More Quiet Pleasure from Barbara Pym." *Cleveland Plain Dealer,* 11 July, p. 16.
Review of *An Unsuitable Attachment*. Notes that Pym has "a rare touch among writers, sly and kind, amusing and sober."

60 STALEY, THOMAS F. "The Inside Story." *Tulsa Home and Garden,* April, p. 17.
Brief review of *Jane and Prudence*. Comments on Pym's small and familiar world, but "no less knowing and deeply moving" than Gail Godwin's. Pym's writing is marked by "deep human sympathy and understanding."

61 SUTTON, JUDITH. "Fiction." *Library Journal* 107 (15 May):1012.
Brief review of *An Unsuitable Attachment*. "While not quite so sharply focused as other of Pym's novels, this is still a finely drawn and witty novel."

62 _____. "Fiction." *Library Journal* 107 (15 December):2353.
Review of *No Fond Return of Love*. Calls this one of Pym's "most amusing" novels and Dulcie Mainwaring "an endearing" heroine.

63 SWARTLEY, ARIEL. "Barbara Pym's Cup of Tea." *Boston Phoenix,* 20 July, sec. 3, p. 6.
Review of *An Unsuitable Attachment*. The characters' lives are "neither narrower nor less eventful" than those in classic English novels, "though with her devastatingly bland understatement . . . Pym is perhaps a more self-effacing observer." This quietness makes her very much "an Anglophile's cup of tea."

64 TOULSON, SHIRLEY. "Fiction." *British Book News,* June, p. 385.
Review of *An Unsuitable Attachment*. As a "fitting summary" of Pym's early work, this novel's "high spirits come from a witty mixture of the sensual and the ecclesiastical." Pym observes her characters with the "shrewd, detached yet affectionate eye of the anthropologist."

65 TYLER, ANNE. "Symposium: Books That Gave Me Pleasure." *New York Times Book Review,* 5 December, p. 48.

Lists Barbara Pym as "Jane Austen reincarnated." Wonders whom readers will turn to when they've finished with Pym.

66 WELTY, EUDORA. "Symposium: Books That Gave Me Pleasure." *New York Times Book Review,* 5 December, p. 48.

Pym's best novels *(Excellent Women, A Glass of Blessings, Less Than Angels)* are "sheer delight, and all of them companionable. Quiet, paradoxical, funny and sad, they have the iron in them of permanence too."

67 WILLISON, MARILYN MURRAY. "Amour of Lady to the Mannerly Born." *Los Angeles Times Book Review,* 22 July, p. 26.

Review of *An Unsuitable Attachment.* Although the novel's plot might be too slow-moving for some readers, its "quiet charm and wry wit should appeal to many." One of Pym's major strengths is her ability to toss off "pointed descriptions."

68 WILSON, A.N. "St. Barbara-in-the-Precinct." *Spectator* 248 (20 February):22-23.

Review of *An Unsuitable Attachment.* Those who compare Pym to Jane Austen miss the latter's "total absence of malice. ... Few novelists' eyes have ever observed the lonely ludicrousness of human existence more acutely than she did." The latest novel is up to Pym's "usual standard" and "rich" in all that we have come to expect of her. Focuses on her characters' "quiet courage" and preoccupations with food. Reviews the publishing history of her latest novel, explains why he feels that Jonathan Cape turned the book down unfairly, and quotes Tom Maschler who gives his version of the novel's earlier rejection. Excerpted: 1982.49; Reprinted: 1988.32.

69 ZINMAN, JANE. "Early Pym Novel Shows Signs of Emerging Talent." *Columbus Sunday Dispatch,* 4 April, p. 19.

Review of *Jane and Prudence.* Finds here the earmarks of vintage Pym, but in "a rough and spotty form." Says that the "finer sense of discrimination of the mature writer" has not yet developed. "Nonetheless, it is a pleasant enough tale, and interesting for the light it sheds on the development of this fine English novelist."

1983

1 ALLEN, BRUCE. "Browsing." *Chicago Tribune Book World,* 1 May, p. 2.
     Brief review of *No Fond Return of Love.* Calls Dulcie Mainwaring a "vintage Pym creation" and this a "novel of education," clever and entertaining.

2 ANON. "Books for Vacation Reading: Fiction." *New York Times Book Review,* 12 June, p. 36.
     Brief review of *No Fond Return of Love.* Like her other novels, seems "drawn from the daydreams of refreshingly sensible women [and] reminds us of the heartbreaking silliness of daily life."

3 ANON. "Briefly Noted: Fiction." *New Yorker* 58 (17 January):112-13.
     Review of *No Fond Return of Love.* Pym "vent[s] her love of the ludicrous" on an assortment of unusual minor characters. The heroine in this "wonderful comedy" with a complicated plot is "inimitable [and] unforgettable."

4 ANON. "Briefly Noted: Fiction." *New Yorker* 59 (5 September):112.
     Brief review of *Some Tame Gazelle.* Only Pym heroines could think the thoughts and consider the wonders that concern this pair of "slightly dotty, utterly contrary middle-aged country spinsters."

5 ANON. "Browsing." *Chicago Tribune Book World,* 1 May, p. 2.
     Brief review of *No Fond Return of Love.* In this "novel of education" once again Pym entertains with a story about the war between men and women, "a civilized exchange of discreet reconnoiterings and finely phrased hostilities."

6 ANON. "Cross Currents." *Publishers Weekly* 224 (5 August):16.
     Notice that a plaque to commemorate the life of Pym will soon be installed in the Holy Trinity Church at Finstock, Oxfordshire, the village in which she lived the last seven years of her life.

7 ANON. "Fiction." *Kirkus Reviews.* 51 (1 June):634-35.
     Review of *Some Tame Gazelle.* This "upbeat little diversion" lacks the high comedy of "prime Pym" or the pathos of "late Pym," but offers "a nice blend of light and sharp, pitch-perfect when it comes to charity concerts, genteel put-downs, and serene self-deceptions."

8 ANON. "Notes on Current Books: Fiction." *Virginia Quarterly Review* 59 (Winter):18, 20.

Mention of *An Unsuitable Attachment*. Pym's "understated style" is appropriate for describing the relationships between unmarried men and women whose "quiet lives are filled with humdrum tasks and petty social obligations."

9 ANON. "Paperback Choice." *Observer* (London), 10 April, p. 31.

Review of *An Unsuitable Attachment*. "Pym's distressed spinsters, canons' widows, curates, and the [l]ike, couldn't have asked for a wittier fictional anthropologist." Calls the novel "pleasingly wry."

10 ANON. "PW Forecasts: Fiction." *Publishers Weekly* 223 (10 June):55-56.

Review of *Some Tame Gazelle*. This "diverting tale" will only "mildly amuse" those readers familiar with the subtle wit in Pym's later works. Although not Pym's most sophisticated and insightful novel, "it marked an auspicious debut."

11 BAYLEY, JOHN. "Life-Enhancing World-Views." *Times Literary Supplement*, 16 September, p. 978.

Compares Pym's work with Jane Austen's.

12 B[ELL], H[AZEL] K. "Indexers in Fiction." *Indexer* 13 (3 April):198.

Comments on the appearance of indexers in *Excellent Women, Less Than Angels,* and *Jane and Prudence* and recommends all of her novels to readers interested in the subject. Not only do indexers appear, "but characters from each story make fleeting appearances in subsequent novels, forming a network of allusions, addenda and cross-references to entrance the indexing heart."

13 BENET, DIANA. "Barbara Pym and the Novel of Manners." *Cross Currents* 33 (Winter):4499-501.

Review of *A Few Green Leaves*. This "immensely enjoyable" novel is Pym's most positive depiction of church and clergyman.

14 BINDING, PAUL. "Barbara Pym." In *British Novelists since 1960. Part Two: H-Z.* Vol. 14, *Dictionary of Literary Biography.* Edited by Jay L. Halio. Detroit: Gale, pp. 604-7.

Offers an overview of Pym's life, character, and career from *Some Tame Gazelle* through *A Few Green Leaves*. "At its best [her] fiction combines, in an extraordinarily intricate way, the interior and the exterior."

15 BITKER, MARJORIE. "A Tea-Time Treat from Pym." *Milwaukee Journal,* 9 January, p. 26.

Review of *No Fond Return of Love.* All of these distinct characters are motivated by their search for true love. Of all the journeys taken, the most impressive is the one into the interior of Dulcie Mainwaring herself, "who is always honest and refuses to settle for second best." Calls this "a charming, witty, utterly beguiling story."

16 B[LAMIRES], H[ARRY], ed. "Pym, Barbara (1913-1980)." In *A Guide to Twentieth Century Literature in English.* London and New York: Methuen, pp. 227-28.

Brief biographical background and discussion of *No Fond Return of Love, The Sweet Dove Died, Quartet in Autumn,* and *A Few Green Leaves.*

17 BROYARD, ANATOLE. "A Funnier Jane Austen." *New York Times,* 1 January, p. 12.

Review of *No Fond Return of Love.* Says that Pym is funnier than Jane Austen and that "she works more on the fringes of society." Her characters' "irrepressible honesty" is also quite different from Austen's "aggressive, hurtful kind." Notes a similarity between Pym and her heroine, Dulcie Mainwaring: "one of those rare women who sees through people without feeling superior to them."

18 BURKHART, CHARLES. "Barbara Pym and the Africans." *Twentieth Century Literature* 29 (Spring):45-53.

Examines the influences of anthropology in all of her novels. Out of her background, her job, her lovers, and her friends she made "her formal comedies, thoughtful and moving, hilarious and serene. . . . She has made Africa come home to suburbia and found that they are the same, and in such a discovery some of her genius lies." Includes biographical details.

19 _____. "A 1st Novel Highlights the Revival of an Author's Work." *Philadelphia Inquirer Books/Leisure,* 7 August, p. 2.

Review of *Some Tame Gazelle.* Finds Pym's world both quiet and funny. "But she is less severe than Jane Austen, morally less judgmental; her range is smaller and her texture less coarse than Trollope's; she is not cozy or sentimental like Mrs. Gaskell." Calls the novel "unquenchably droll and ironic [with] all the charm of great beginnings."

20 CALDWELL, MARGARET. "Some News of Our Country Cousins from Barbara Pym." *Cleveland Plain Dealer,* 28 August, p. D4.

Review of *Some Tame Gazelle.* Uninitiated Pym readers of her first novel will wonder why this rediscovered author has attracted so much attention; the scale here is even smaller than in her later works. But the "Pym aficionado" will be very much at home with this story. "[T]he sisters are depicted so engagingly, if not uncritically, that the effect is like that of a letter from a country cousin: Small joys and disappointments matter, because you care about the people involved."

21 CASEY, CONSTANCE. "Very British, Very Charming." *USA Today,* 22 July, p. 4D.

Review of *Some Tame Gazelle.* Comments on the "comfortingly familiar" narrow world and stock characters and the pleasure to be received from Pym's witty observations. Predicts a wide audience for this book because of Pym's "distinctive combination of hardheaded acumen and warm sympathy."

22 CRAIG, PATRICIA. "In Brief." *Times Literary Supplement,* 1 July, p. 711.

Brief review of *An Unsuitable Attachment.* Calls it "adroit and agreeable."

23 DONAHUE, DEIRDRE. "More Social Comedy from Barbara Pym." *Cleveland Plain Dealer,* 13 February, p. 11.

Review of *No Fond Return of Love.* Comments on similarities between this novel and Pym's other works. Usually her heroines search for a purpose in life, sometimes finding it in religion, often experiencing loneliness in their tidy little flats. "Pym renders these desolate moments with compassion, and recognizes that they sometimes occur as one pours out a single cup of midnight Ovaltine."

24 DUFFY, MARTHA. "In Praise of Excellent Women." *Time* 122 (26 September):70.

Overview of Pym's career: "patience rewarded, prevalence over adversity." Discusses her characters, world, church, interest in anthropology, and comedy as well as notes "a harder side" to Pym: "an acute knowledge of the heart's foolishness, of the forces that isolate and diminish the aging, of the helplessness of the poor and the unlucky to alter the course of their lives." Throughout her novels she was "strictly true to what she knew."

25 DYER, RICHARD. "Pym's Comedic Skill Makes Quiet Happenings Reverberate." *Boston Globe,* 31 July, p. 24.

   Review of *Some Tame Gazelle.* Discusses Pym's "quiet comedy," from which slowly emerges "little joys and great silent sorrows." Pym unobtrusively dramatizes the gap between them.

26 EPSTEIN, JOSEPH. "Sex and the Single Novel." *Hudson Review* 36 (Spring):185-86.

   Review of *No Fond Return of Love.* Finds similarities between Pym and the Reverend Sydney Smith, "who once advised a friend suffering from depression, among other things, to keep good blazing fires, be as busy as you can, attend to the effects coffee and tea produce upon you, and take short views of human life." Calls Pym a comedian "who can make one care about her comic creations." *Quartet in Autumn,* on the other hand, is "quite terrifying."

27 EZELL, MARGARET [J.M.] "Pym: An 'Excellent Woman.' " *Houston Chronicle,* 9 October, p. 15.

   Review of *Some Tame Gazelle.* Because of their efforts to prove or disprove similarities with Jane Austen, many readers have overlooked what Pym actually is: "a wry, sensitive observer of her society, with a wicked sense of absurdities in even the most placid life and the literary skill to plant her finely crafted ironic barbs effortlessly on target."

28 FULLER, EDMUND. "Two Remaining Works of a Novelist of the Ordinary." *Wall Street Journal,* 18 July, p. 18.

   Review of *Some Tame Gazelle* and *No Fond Return of Love.* Like Jane Austen, Pym is able "to engage us in the muted but intensely real dramas in the lives of genteel middle-class people." Her observations are acute and often very funny, sometimes tart but never malicious.

29 GOLD, EDITH. "Fiction in Brief." *Miami Herald,* 27 November, p. E7.

   Brief review of *Some Tame Gazelle.* Like Pym's other novels, this one is "perceptive, kindly, rather churchy, and hilarious."

30 _____. "Pym's Cup Runneth Over." *Miami Herald,* 27 February, p. E9.

   Brief review of *No Fond Return of Love.* Notes Pym's "piercing eye and sharp wit," her characters' "mild" adventures, and her interest in the Church of England.

31 GORRA, MICHAEL. "Restraint Is the Point." *New York Times Book Review,* 31 July, pp. 12, 18.
   Review of *Some Tame Gazelle.* The big moments here are "quiet, offhand realizations presented without a trace of bravado, as if they were accidents." Like Jane Austen, Pym has a "compressed and seemingly casual way of letting her characters unwittingly reveal themselves." Praises the novel as having "all the quiet skill, the tough, reasonable wit and, above all, the calm integrity of [her] best work." Notes occasional lapses into the woman's page idiom and awkward references to foreign literature, philosophy, and other esoteric matters. Excerpted: 1986.43.

32 H[OOPER], W[ILLIAM] B[RADLEY]. "Fiction." *Booklist* 79 (15 May):1166.
   Review of *Some Tame Gazelle.* Calls Pym "exquisitely charming" as she pokes "gentle fun" at her characters' distress over small issues. "The theme is entirely and most refreshingly positive: that despite upsets, regularity in one's existence can triumph and the future loom comfortably par."

33 JOHNSTON, MARGUERITE. "Glimpses of a Pym and Proper World." *Houston Post,* 23 January, p. F24.
   Review of *No Fond Return of Love* and *Jane and Prudence.* "The fun is quiet, more of a twinkle at the predictable things people say and do, with moments of recognition and kinship." Hers is "a world of nice-mindedness."

34 _____. "More Pym, Proper Humor." *Houston Post,* 11 September, p. 19.
   Review of *Some Tame Gazelle.* Finds delight in this novel "perhaps her funniest" for its "gentle, ironic sketch of life" in an English village. None of the characters sees his own absurdity or the comedy around him. "Only the author and the reader can see the fun."

35 JONES, SUSAN CURVIN. "If You Don't Know Barbara Pym. . . ." *Minneapolis Tribune,* 25 September, p. G15.
   Review of *Some Tame Gazelle.* People read Pym because she can write. "In her facile hands, the most mundane characters and events are transformed by wit, compassion, irony and consummate control into art." Finds in her first novel "all the hallmarks of her unique talents" and typical conclusion of "a celebration of the commonplace."

36 KAKUTANI, MICHIKO. "Books of the Times." *New York Times,* 5 August, p. 19.

Review of *Some Tame Gazelle.* In this "lovely, muted novel," Pym skillfully causes the reader not only to care about what happens but also to experience the significance of everyday events. Comments on the author's voice ("steady and quietly assured"), themes (perils of love, tendency to form unsuitable attachments), and emotions ("palpable and real"). This novel suggests that Pym had grasped her subject and her style from the very start of her career.

37 KAPP, ISA. "One Woman's Virtue." *Washington Post Book World,* 14 June, p. 12.

Review of *No Fond Return of Love.* Considers the setting, wisdom, and comedy, and concludes that the novel is "a shade more rueful than her typical fiction." Excerpted: 1986.43.

38 ____. "Out of the Swim with Barbara Pym." *American Scholar* 52 (Spring):237-42.

Appreciates Pym's novels as a "sanctuary from the enormous liberties and vast territory" often found in modern fiction. Considers her settings ("comfortably confining"), heroines ("dignified anachronisms" and superior to men), humor (sometimes tongue in cheek), precise observation of speech, manner, and mentality ("awesome"), plots ("startlingly narrow"), voice (calm but contributing to suspense), allusions to poetry, and universal appeal. Concludes that beneath Pym's extraordinary forbearance and compassion there is "a layer of sheer spinal firmness and imperturbable detachment that puts her into the rank of first-rate novelists." Along with that detachment, finds an "ability to see several things at the same time."

39 ____. "The Terrifying World of Plain People in Love." *Los Angeles Herald-Examiner,* 30 January, p. F6.

Review of *No Fond Return of Love.* In the world of modern fiction, Pym is "a lone sturdy figure, bent on making virtue entertaining." Finds the setting in this novel to be "more confined" than in her other works, with little of the "congenial church bustle [and] a shade more rueful." Pym's honesty contributes a "terrifying element" to her writing.

40 KING, NINA. "Humorous and Gentle Country Loves." *Newsday,* 27 July, p. 11.

Review of *Some Tame Gazelle.* Says that the comedy here is "shadowed by a certain poignance and wistfulness." Its title suggests the "quiet yearning" of Pym's aging heroines.

41 KISSELL, HOWARD. "Books." *Women's Wear Daily,* 27 July, p. 13.
Review of *Some Tame Gazelle.* Calls the world in this novel "very Trollopean." Part of her appeal is that her world is timeless and "not overburdened by change." Recommends *No Fond Return of Love,* too.

42 LARSON, EDITH S. "The Celebration of the Ordinary in Barbara Pym's Novels." *San Jose Studies* 9, no. 2:17-22.
Offers an overview of Pym's novels through *An Unsuitable Attachment.*

43 LEIGHTON, BETTY. "Ah, What Pym Can Do with a Meager Plot." *Winston-Salem* (N.C.) *Journal,* 20 February, p. C4.
Review of *No Fond Return of Love.* Calls this a "minor masterpiece, a perfectly balanced novel." Discusses Pym's playfulness. Once again she has entertained us "richly" and "deepened our sensibilities" toward English middle-class life.

44 LEVY, BARBARA. "Books." *Sunday San Juan Star Magazine,* 10 October, p. 4.
Review of *Some Tame Gazelle.* Renewed interest in Pym is well founded. Praises this book for its "wry observations of human weaknesses" and notes similarities among all of her novels.

45 _____. "Why Study Literature? Women on Literature/Women in Literature: A Dialogue." *Sunday San Juan Star Magazine,* 10 October, pp. 2-4.
Three graduate students in Puerto Rico defend the study of English literature in a Spanish-speaking, technological society. Joan Rullan, for example, selected Barbara Pym as her thesis topic.

46 LOBRANO, ALEXANDER. "Pym's Cup Now Overflows." *Gentleman's Quarterly,* May, p. 37.
Overview of Pym's life and career. "Amidst the hundreds of cups of tea upon which her plots float, there's an extraordinary humor – wry and discreetly informing, very English in its economy – that serves as the background for the gentle, mannered lives of her characters." Mentions her characters' wit and self-control as well as their instinctive respect for the rule of moral behavior and their relationships.

1983

47 MAITRE, DOREEN. *Literature and Possible Worlds*. Hamden, Conn.: Shoe String Press, pp. 14-17.

   Considers *Quartet in Autumn* as an example of fiction that affects the lives of its readers.

48 MARSH, PAMELA. "Pym's First Novel Is Finally in Print Stateside." *Christian Science Monitor,* 7 October, p. 9.

   Review of *Some Tame Gazelle*. Pym turns her "shrewd, mocking, but always affectionate eye" on English country life thirty years ago. Harriet and Belinda Bede lead "Jane Austenlike lives." One of Pym's favorite themes, love, has nothing to do with sex and "flourishes only when it is hopeless."

49 MILLER, ELLEN J. (producer). "Barbara Pym: Out of the Wilderness." Belmont, Mass.: Greybirch Productions. Videotape.

   Portrait of Pym, recorded on her seventieth birthday on 2 June 1983 at her cottage in New Oxford. Includes rare footage obtained from a BBC interview (1977) and an interview (1983) with Hilary Pym and Hazel Holt.

50 NIEMTZOW, ANNETTE. "Pym: Old-Fashioned and Sweet but Not an Equal of Jane Austen." *Philadelphia Inquirer,* 6 February, p. 7.

   Review of *No Fond Return of Love*. Praises the novel's "lightness and control" and "gentle wit" as reminiscent of a Victorian novel. Both the book and the characters are "unfailingly, even embarrassingly, self-conscious."

51 OVERMYER, JANET. "Pym's First Novel Fine." *Columbus Sunday Dispatch,* 28 August, p. 13.

   Review of *Some Tame Gazelle*. Finds here "delightful humor" but not in as great an abundance as in the later books.

52 OWINGS, ALISON. "Bridled Passions in an English Village." *San Francisco Chronicle Book Review,* 21 August, p. 1.

   Brief review of *Some Tame Gazelle*.

53 PEYTON, GEORGINA. "Main Street, England." *San Diego Union Books,* 24 July, p. 6.

   Review of *Some Tame Gazelle*. With a sure hand Pym cuts through her characters' small hypocrisies, revealing them both as they think they are and as they really are. Pym's comedic talent makes the supper party at the vicarage "a gem of an occasion."

54 QUINN, MARY ELLEN. "Fiction." *Library Journal* 108 (July):1383.
    Review of *Some Tame Gazelle.* "Nothing dramatic happens: the novel's interest lies in Pym's close observation of her characters and their ordinary lives."

55 ROBACK, DIANE, and ALLENE SYMONS. "Bookstore Summer Sales Are Up." *Publishers Weekly* 224 (2 September):52.
    Mentions the phenomenal renewed interest in Pym's books. One bookstore manager in Chicago said, "Barbara Pym has been selling like water on a hot iron; her books just disappear."

56 R[OCHMIS], D[OROTHY] H. "Fiction." *West Coast Review of Books* 9 (January):29.
    Brief review of *No Fond Return of Love.* Pym's narrative is "charming and delightful" as she writes with "tongue-in-cheek" of her characters' mores.

57 RUBIN, MERLE. "For Anglophiles, Pym's Number One." *Los Angeles Herald-Examiner,* 28 August, pp. F5-F6.
    Review of *Some Tame Gazelle.* Although comic, Pym's heroines are capable of self-knowledge. Their gentility makes their erotic aspirations seem "more daring." Like Jane Austen, Pym is able to make the quiet lives of unremarkable characters seem interesting. "[O]nly a writer of comic genius can view the petty pace of the daily round with a blend of irony and sympathy that magnifies the pathos of the very subjects it lovingly mocks."

58 SALWAK, DALE. "Barbara Pym." In *Critical Survey of Long Fiction.* Edited by Frank N. Magill. Englewood Cliffs, N.J.: Salem Press, pp. 2178-85.
    Offers an overview of Pym's life and career as well as an analysis of *Excellent Women, A Glass of Blessings,* and *Quartet in Autumn.* "Each novel is a miniature work of art, distinguished by an air of assurance, an easy but firm control of the material, and the economy of means to achieve it."

59 SEE, CAROLYN. "Romance: Does It Last or Does It Lust?" *Los Angeles Times,* 16 August, pt. V, p. 6
    Review of *Some Tame Gazelle.* Calls this "pure gold." Says that the only reality here is "dinner, and romance, and gossip, the gentle excitement of what's going to happen next, and wicked, wicked scenes between the archdeacon and the bishop that makes [the reader] laugh out loud."

60 SHAPIRO, ANNA. "The Resurrection of Barbara Pym." *Saturday Review* 9 (July/August):29-31.

Looks at the renewed interest in Pym's novels and considers John Updike's assessment (*see* 1983.67). "Today something like Pym-mania has struck the literary world, justifying her classification as 'permanent.' " Looks at the first ten novels and considers her themes, her devotion to the church, her humility ("a kind of clarity of spirit"), and her shift toward realism. "Barbara Pym's life exemplifies the maxim that the last shall be first and the first shall be last."

61 SORENSEN, ROBERT. "Index This One under 'D'–for 'Delightful.' " *Minneapolis Tribune,* 16 January, p. G13.

Review of *No Fond Return of Love.* Had avoided Pym for years because he assumed that she was a "literary sister" of Barbara Cartland. This novel proves how wrong he was. "[It] is all very British, full of ingratiating events and characters."

62 STEWART, SUSAN. "Passion vs. Poetry in Pym's 'Gazelle.' " *Dallas Times Herald,* 2 October, p. 9.

Review of *Some Tame Gazelle.* Pym is an entertaining novelist, a "sly comedian." Her point in this novel is that "nothing happens." Although the sisters are not as complex as later Pym characters, "they are finely drawn, and there's not a false note."

63 STROUSE, JEAN. "Tempest in a Teacup." *Newsweek* 101 (24 January):68.

Review of *No Fond Return of Love.* "Pym brilliantly fixes people inside their illusions and self-deceptions, but her vision is generous rather than harshly satiric." Calls the plot "spicy, rich and warmly satisfying."

64 TALIAFERRO, FRANCES. "Fiction." *Harper's* 267 (August):74-75.

Review of *Some Tame Gazelle.* With a few exceptions, Pym's world is "clement and comfortable" and her characters are timeless. Part of the pleasure derived from reading her novels is that the characters behave "exactly as they are expected to." In the characterization of the sisters and in the "ironic symmetries of its gentle plot," this novel often echoes Jane Austen. Pym also shares with Trollope a gift for "distinguishing and choreographing a large cast of characters" and with Angela Thirkell, "a sense of humor that alternates between donnish wordplay and a giddy appreciation of the ridiculous." But Pym is herself, and in this entertaining novel she has created two characters who are "intelligent, contented, and good." Excerpted: 1986.43.

65 TYLER, ANNE. "From England to West Virginia." *New York Times Book Review,* 13 February, pp. 1, 22.

Review of *No Fond Return of Love.* Refers to Pym's "refreshingly sensible and not obviously beautiful" men and women, noting parallels with Jane Austen. But whereas Austen's men are worth the trouble to pursue, Pym's men are "vain and pretentious." Character is everything in her novels. The themes are "more certain" in this novel. Pym is "the rarest of treasures; she reminds us of the heartbreaking silliness of daily life." Excerpted: 1986.43.

66 UPDIKE, JOHN. *Hugging the Shore: Essays and Criticism.* New York: Knopf, pp. 516, 519-25.

Reprint of 1979.28.

67 _____. "Letters" *Saturday Review* 101 (September/October):10.

Responds to Anna Shapiro's misrepresentation of his views on Pym (*see* 1983.60).

68 VOGEL, CHRISTINE B. "A Sip of Pym's Number One." *Washington Post Book World,* 21 August, pp. 1, 14.

Review of *Some Tame Gazelle.* Pym gives her characters importance. "She shows us their thinking, details their small comforts, exposes their essential solitude, all without sentimentality." Excerpted: 1986.43.

69 WEST, MARTHA ULLMAN. "Profile: Barbara Pym." *San Francisco Review of Books* 7 (March/April):21-22.

Brief biographical background and overview of Pym's career.

70 WILSON, JOHN. "An Unsuitable Attachment." In *Magill's Literary Annual 1983.* Edited by Frank A. Magill. Englewood Cliffs, N.J.: Salem Press, pp. 855-59.

The recurring characters and other devices and motifs in *An Unsuitable Attachment* invite "the reader to share and delight in the making of a fictional world." Although fitting into the sequence of her novels, its atypical features suggest that Pym was "in the process of changing direction." Praises the novel for its metafictionist's techniques and its "rich gallery of minor characters, its felicity of phrase, its delightful cameos of characters from earlier novels in the sequence, its rendering of the strangeness of everyday life."

71 ZUCKERMAN, AMY. "In Brief." *Sunday Telegraph* (London), 16 January, p. 8E.

Brief review of *No Fond Return of Love*. Pym seems to be "groping for realism," but unable to break away entirely from the "overly optimistic" conventions of an earlier time. In spite of its many charming moments, the novel doesn't "hang together" as well as some of her earlier books.

72 ____. "Vintage First Novel." *Worcester* (Mass.) *Telegram,* 25 September, p. 17.

Review of *Some Tame Gazelle*. "At her best, Miss Pym can bring us deep inside the hopes and aspirations of ordinary people without losing her perspective as narrator, or her well-honed sense of humor," all of which she does "admirably" in this novel.

1984

1 ABEL, BETTY. "Barbara Pym: Novelist and Diarist." *Contemporary Review* 245 (November):278.

Review of *A Very Private Eye*. Finds shining here "a generous good nature which, if one had not read the Angela Thirkell-like novels with their malicious exposé of middle-class values, might appear to be the virtue of a simple soul. In a sense, she is avenged in this delightful volume."

2 ABLEY, MARK. "A Writer's Resurrection." *MacLean's* 97 (27 August):50.

Review of *A Very Private Eye*. Like her fiction, this book "displays ample evidence of Pym's tendency to mingle great and tiny issues" and contains "a host of vignettes that seem inimitably English." Includes an overview of her career.

3 ACKROYD, PETER. "Manufacturing Miss Pym." *Times Literary Supplement,* 3 August, p. 861.

Review of *A Very Private Eye*. Pym remains something of a mystery that this compilation does little to fathom. However, in addition to the blandness of her life as it is presented here, notes that another Pym emerges from these pages almost by accident – that of a "single-minded, almost obsessive, woman." Her ability or need to dramatize herself gives "that peculiar flavour to her writing, in which intimacy and detachment are subtly commingled, in which banality of self-identification and the brilliance of her thoroughly cold gaze are dissembled in comedy."

4 ANON. "Barbara Pym's Journals to Be Published by Dutton." *Book Alert,* June, p. 9.

Brief mention of *A Very Private Eye* with biographical details.

5 ANON. "Books: Fiction." *West Coast Review of Books,* February, p. 15.

Brief review of *Some Tame Gazelle.* Her characters "enchant" the reader; her "lively and witty" narrative draws the reader into the village life routine.

6 ANON. "Briefly Noted: General." *New Yorker* 60 (16 July):91-92.

Review of *A Very Private Eye.* Finds in the diaries "the essential Barbara Pym: Curious and wry, and always gathering, sometimes grimly, grist for her mill." Part 1 is "especially rich in comic characters."

7 ANON. "Browsing." *Chicago Tribune,* 12 August, sec. 14, p. 39.

Brief review of *A Very Private Eye.* In this "delightful pastiche" the reader will find "the same little ironies and attention to small detail" that distinguish the novels.

8 ANON. "Fiction." *Kirkus Reviews* 52 (15 May):486.

Review of *A Very Private Eye.* This "very uneven, ultimately unsatisfying" compilation is likely "to enchant some cultists and perplex some others, while more discriminating Pym admirers will be only intermittently engaged."

9 ANON. "Fiction." *Kirkus Reviews* 52 (1 September):814.

In a review of Elizabeth Jolley's *Miss Peabody's Inheritance,* calls the writer "a faintly nasty, slightly smug Barbara Pym – viewing the lonely lines and skewed passions of aging spinsters with cutting irony, condescending pity, but little of Pym's empathy or dignity."

10 ANON. "Holiday Gift Books." *New Directions for Women* 13 (November/December):20.

Recommends *A Very Private Eye* as a "valuable companion" to the novels.

11 ANON. "The New Republic's Best Books." *New Republic* 190 (16 July):46.

Cites *A Very Private Eye* as one of the best books of the year. "The trial and triumphs of a novelist named one of the most underrated writers of the century."

12 ANON. "Newly Discovered Pym Novel Due from Dutton." *Publishers Weekly* 226 (12 October):27.

Interview with Hazel Holt in which notice is given of the forthcoming publication of *Crampton Hodnet* and a collection of Pym's shorter writings.

13 ANON. "Notebook." *New Republic* 191 (27 August):10.

Notes that in *A Very Private Eye* the chapters on Pym's youth are "disfigured by an immature enthusiasm for the German things of Hitler's Germany. ... [G]iven the moral prestige that has been conferred upon her proud provincialism, it is worth noting that her judgment began badly."

14 ANON. "PW Forecasts: Nonfiction." *Publishers Weekly* 225 (4 May):46.

Review of *A Very Private Eye*. Finds here "the repressed emotional fervor that makes her novels so tender, heartwarming and heartbreaking. ... Recorded are events of daily life her readers will reveal in and recognize as archetypally 'Pym.' " The diaries leave us "knowing Pym and loving her."

15 ANON. "Pym's Number One." *Economist* 292 (1 September):73-74.

Review of *A Very Private Eye*. "Admirers will be grateful to have this background against which to place her work."

16 ANON. "Women." *Fiction, Literature and the Arts Review* 34 (Spring):32.

Review of *Some Tame Gazelle*. In this novel Pym is at "her most decadent and riotous best, and the satire . . . is equal to the intensity of any comic fiction." Attributes her growing appeal to "the deft handling of her prose, . . . the seamless structure of her plots and, above all, . . . the honesty of her values."

17 BAILEY, PAUL. "Smiling Through." *Observer Review,* 22 July, p. 20.

Review of *A Very Private Eye*. Calls this the "perfect compliment" to Pym's fiction – "a celebration in itself of the everyday ironies . . . she made her concern." Includes biographical details.

18 BAYLEY, JOHN. "Barbara Pym: Sharp Clarity and Cosy Obscurity." *Harpers Queen,* July, p. 142.

Review of *A Very Private Eye*. Notes the connections between her life and novels: her sense of enjoyment with the small pleasures of life, her "marvellous" sense of humor about the relations between the sexes, her honesty about what it is like to be a woman. "No one conveys better the commonplace thrills of being in love, and what one associates with it." This compilation reads "as funnily, and as movingly, as one of her novels."

19 BENET, DIANA. "The Language of Christianity in Pym's Novels." *Thought* 59 (December):504-13.

Considers all ten novels and notes that Pym writes with "an affectionate irreverence" that is reminiscent of the Barchester novels at their best, calling attention to the contemporary situation of the church. Her topics include "the pious cliché, religious phrases, hymns, prayer, and the clerical voice (especially in sermons). These, together with the themes of the Church as social organization and of the embarrassment of religious commitment, outline a coherent vision." All along she emphasizes the need for the church to do "its unique work." Only *The Sweet Dove Died* does not center on the church and the Anglican clergy.

20 BILLINGTON, RACHEL. "Spinster Eye." *Financial Times* (London), 21 July, p. 23.

Review of *A Very Private Eye*. Offers an "unemotional estimate" of Pym's work, which is helped by the publication of her diaries and journals, "well-written and entertaining on a rather more dramatic scale than her novels." Finds that her books turn out to be "a pale imitation of what she actually felt." Missing from her life and work are any signs of "spiritual succour (or lack of it)." And yet beneath the writing lurks "the passionate woman" that gives her fictional characters a "secret sexuality," which has made her books a favourite. She has always been fascinated by the concept of the spinster.

21 BROOKNER, ANITA. "High Spirit." *Standard* (London), 18 July, p. 13.

Review of *A Very Private Eye*. Finds here "an honest and sweet-tempered woman . . . whose regrets were all the more painful in that they seemed so unnecessary." As a writer, she was "easy and natural, although not necessarily what is called a born writer." The collection reveals her "living essence." Excerpted: 1984.80.

22 BROYARD, ANATOLE. "Books of the Times." *New York Times,* 14 June, p. 21.

Review of *A Very Private Eye*. Finds here all the "quietly remarkable qualities" that caused the publishing world to reverse itself about her. It is ironic that she was rejected both by lovers and by publishers "because she was too good for them and not exciting enough in a superficial way. Her excitement ran too deep and was too pure for a nervous age."

23 BUNKE, JOAN. "Miss Pym to the Life." *Des Moines Sunday Register,* 19 August, p. 18.
    Review of *A Very Private Eye.* This collection is full of "rich material – pithy dialogues, witty turns of phrase, discreet but explicit sexuality, and much literary matter," including some letters written in the style of Gertrude Stein.

24 C., J. "Two Enduring Works by Women Novelists." *Los Angeles Federal Savings Quarterly,* Winter, p. 43.
    Review of *Some Tame Gazelle,* calling it "a shrewd, cunning and compassionate view of life in an English village." Finds similarities between Pym and the novelist, Elizabeth Taylor: "the deft and precise realism of their work, an ironic detachment and utter lack of sentimentality."

25 CAREY, JOHN. "Pym's Little Ironies." *Sunday Times* (London), 22 July, p. 12.
    Review of *A Very Private Eye.* The compilation shows "life shading into fiction" right before our eyes. Food, clothes, and graves are her "staple enthusiasms." Though lacking the "shapeliness of her novels," these diaries and notebooks are a "remarkably good substitute."

26 CLAYTON, SYLVIA. "Portrait of a Miniaturist." *Daily Telegraph* (London), 20 July, p. 6.
    Review of *A Very Private Eye.* Comments on Pym's comedy, style ("prudent"), moods (at times dejected, but never bitter), courage, and modesty. Calls her an "alert miniaturist [who] drew civilised comedy from the foibles and worries of Anglican clergy and their wives, civil servants and displaced spinsters." Her ten novels are instantly recognizable for their "distinctive flavour." Excerpted: 1984.80.

27 CLEMONS, WALTER. "A Quiet Life Full of Surprises." *Newsweek* 104 (23 July):64.
    Review of *A Very Private Eye.* For anyone who has experienced "the subtle, precise charm" of Pym's novels, this collection will be of "considerable appeal." Finds it "startling" to meet the young Pym as a romantic; later, her "sturdiness of character" emerges as does her "witty, likable" character.

28 COLE, THOMAS. "Pym, the Heart-on-Sleeve Spinster." *Baltimore Evening Sun,* 20 August, p. 17.

Review of *A Very Private Eye.* Finds reflected in the novels "intelligence, keen interest in people, subtle and incisive wit, and a seeming lack of guile or envy." Considers it "amazing" how often Pym's personal life is reflected in her novels.

29 COLEGATE, ISABEL, and MICHAEL DIRDA. "Tea and Sympathy: Philip Larkin and Barbara Pym." *Washington Post Book World,* 1 July, pp. 1, 5.

Review of *A Very Private Eye.* Finds in *Some Tame Gazelle* all the qualities that Pym's admirers cherish: "the eye for the comic details of everyday life, the appreciation of the absurd in human behavior, the acute observation which is unsentimental without being uncharitable." The compilation confirms that Pym was a "remarkably nice woman." Finds here the same voice one hears in her fiction: "sometimes childlike, always good-natured, relishing the ridiculous, hoping for the best." One's taste for her novels grows in the reading of them.

30 CORRIGAN, MAUREEN. "Pym Agonistes." *Village Voice* 29 (31 July):45-46.

Review of *A Very Private Eye.* "As a commentator on her own life, Pym rivals the gossipy, blunt, but excellent women of her imagination."

31 DAHLIN, ROBERT. "How Could I Have Waited So Long, Miss Pym?" *Christian Science Monitor,* 7 December, p. B2.

Overview of Pym's career. Praises her world, her powers of observation, and her humane view of life. Finds on the surface similarities with Jane Austen, but her voice is unique: "outwardly fragile, yet inwardly piercing."

32 DANIEL, MARGARET. "Excellent Woman." *Church Times* (London), 3 August, p. 6.

Review of *A Very Private Eye.* Finds here a "remarkably close" equation between fact and fiction. Although this "mistress of reserve" never retreats from life, in a "curious way" she resembles Emily Dickinson. "People and the passing show absorb her endlessly; and in her highly personal way she is often very funny." Doubts that any further study will be able to match the "felicities of Pym on Pym."

33 DANTO, ARTHUR C. "Our Holiday Lists." *Nation* 239 (22 December):688.

Finds it "thrilling" to read of Pym's rediscovery in *A Very Private Eye.* Is grateful to make "a more direct acquaintance" with her than from the novels alone.

34 DICK, KAY. "The Reluctant Spinster." *Spectator* 253 (18 August):23.
Review of *A Very Private Eye.* Calls this "a loving, tender book, a joyful compensation for those of us who did not have the pleasure of knowing [Pym]." Wonders what extracts were omitted. "A good portrait, it could be so described, of a person open to joy and grief."

35 DINNAGE, ROSEMARY. "Comic, Sad, Indefinite." *New York Review of Books,* 16 August, pp. 15-16.
Review of *A Very Private Eye.* Finds that these "frank and entertaining" diaries both conceal and reveal. Why, for example, did Pym see her own story as "subtle" and "amusing"? Finds here "little sign of introspection and psychological complication." A predominating theme in both the life ("comic and sad and indefinite") and the books is summed up by the title of one of her novels, *No Fond Return of Love.* Excerpted: 1986.43.

36 D[ONAVIN], D[ENISE] P. "Fiction." *Booklist* 80 (1 June):1373.
Review of *A Very Private Eye.* Calls this "a sketchy yet intimate portrait and an irresistible opportunity to seek out the personalities and inspiration" behind Pym's fictional characters.

37 DIXLER, ELSA. "Our Holiday Lists." *Nation* 239 (22 December):686.
"Pym's outer life was ... constrained, but her inner life, as *[A Very Private Eye]* shows, was something else again."

38 DYER, RICHARD. "The 'Real' Barbara Pym." *Boston Globe,* 3 July, p. 11.
Review of *A Very Private Eye.* As one of Pym's best books, this collection reveals that "all the ironic indirections of her novels are responses to the very direct and often unhappy experiences of her life, experiences which she bore with a great gallantry." It reveals the personality of "the 'real' Pym," but better than that, it reveals her character.

39 EPSTEIN, JOSEPH. "What's Left to Shock When Anything Goes?" *New York Times Book Review,* 5 February, p. 14.
Expresses pleasure over the success of Pym in both England and America. "[Pym's] novels seem to be finding a readership of the very best kind—readers who seek in fiction news of the inner life, who seek

solace, who seek the pleasures of a superior imagination at work on the materials of everyday life." Quotes from Larkin's letter sent to Faber & Faber in support of Pym's writings after the firm had rejected one of her last novels.

40 ESPEY, JOHN. "Barbara Pym in Her Own Words." *Los Angeles Herald-Examiner,* 26 August, pp. F5-F6.
    Review of *A Very Private Eye.* Enjoys both the revelations of how Pym transformed "immediate experience into either the future or a different setting" and the "frank history [recording] the plight of the marginal novelist of real quality whose works never quite justify themselves in the cold figures of the publisher's balance sheet." Her story is presented in "absorbing detail with a quiet wit that should bring her new readers."

41 EVERETT, BARBARA. "The Pleasures of Poverty." *London Review of Books,* 6 September, pp. 5-6.
    Review of *A Very Private Eye.* Considers Pym's evolution into a novelist as it is recorded through her diaries. Characterizes her novels as romantic antiromances, containing both irony and skepticism. "Pym's 'private' eye was a style that caught the realities of her social world with an intensity equivalent to that of poetry." Reprinted: 1988.11.

42 EZELL, MARGARET J.M. " 'What Shall We Do with Our Old Maids?': Barbara Pym and the 'Woman Question.' " *International Journal of Women's Studies* 7 (November/December):450-65.
    Although Pym owes a stylistic debt to Jane Austen, thematically her first ten novels are part of a very different tradition–the social protest novels of Charlotte Brontë–that most critics have overlooked. "Pym's satiric approach to middle-class English social rituals makes her a penetrating commentator on a specific issue of it, as vexing today as it was in Brontë's time: the position of the single, self-supporting woman caught in a period with a noticeable imbalance in the sex ratio, while the society itself is still rigidly marriage-oriented." Includes biographical background.

43 FENTON, JAMES. "The Passionate Spinster Who Found Humour." *Times* (London), 19 July, p. 10.
    Review of *A Very Private Eye.* "The gift that produced the novel was being practised in these journals. And that gift was for observing the very irreligious preoccupations of clergy life." Pym has come a long

way, endured many disappointments, and acquired "the art of making a very simple statement which is both painful and funny."

44 FINLAYSON, IAIN. "Portrait of a Born-Again Novelist." *Glasgow Herald,* 1 September, p. 7.

Review of *A Very Private Eye.* Calls Pym an "artificial writer, a dandyist of the school of Firbank." This volume reveals much of the raw material she drew from to write her novels, along with "a sharp, ironic, but kindly wit."

45 FISICHELLI, GLYNN-ELLEN MARIA. " 'The Trivial Round, the Common Task.' Barbara Pym: The Development of a Writer." Ph.D. dissertation, State University of New York at Stony Brook, 203 pp.

Examines Pym's development as a writer as well as the parallels between her life and work by analyzing closely her literary notebooks, diaries, comments on writings, and several of her published and unpublished short stories and novels. Focuses on Pym's "method of combining romance fiction conventions with the prosaic details of 'the trivial round, the common task.' " With development come ways of integrating her "autobiographical concerns with fictional ones."

46 FOGARTY, ROBERT S., et al. "Notes by the Editors." *Antioch Review* 42 (Fall):507.

Call *A Very Private Eye* "an intimate and delightfully surprising view" of the author herself. Readers will "cherish" this book.

47 FULLBROOK, KATE. "Fiction." *British Book News,* October, p. 628.

Review of *A Very Private Eye.* "The overwhelming impressions left by this welcome autobiography are of sadness and waste, and of a woman of great talent bravely making do with a far too ordinary life. . . . The sense of frustrations borne with wit and humour, of constantly deepening exasperation, make this book an absorbing study of a life lived with quiet ferocity and a good deal of courage."

48 FULLER, EDMUND. "An Excellent Woman." *Wall Street Journal,* 3 July, p. 22.

Review of *A Very Private Eye.* The more thoroughly one knows the novels, "the greater will be the appreciation of this self-portrait." Finds here "tales of unsuccessful love, wryly wise and never, never dreary."

49 GILL, PENNY. "Getting to Know an Unknown Writer." *Gazette* (Montreal), 4 August, p. I3.

Review of *A Very Private Eye*. In both her novels and her journals, Pym is able "to imbue the most trivial and mundane matters with interest." Her keen eye enables her to render alive "wonderfully ridiculous situations, real or imagined." Also identifies some of Pym's failings: very few memorable characters, little deep analysis of people, a weakness for men who treated her poorly, and a failure to examine how her past influences her present.

50 GLENDINNING, VICTORIA. "Spontaneous Obsessions, Imposed Restraint." *New York Times Book Review*, 8 July, p. 3.
     Review of *A Very Private Eye*. The key to Pym's life and work may well be in her emotional restraint. "It is only the people who are capable, as she always was, of emotional misjudgment on a grand scale, who need to make a point, and finally an art, out of restraint." Pym's "mania for detail" also gives this compilation value as social history. "Her sharp and very private eye never failed her." She is an "extraordinarily accomplished mimic."

51 GRAHAM, ROBERT J. " 'Cumbered with Much Serving: Barbara Pym's *Excellent Women*." *Mosaic* 17 (Spring):141-60.
     Accounts for Pym's renewed popularity through a consideration of her subject matter ("the vagaries of heterosexual relationships") in her first ten novels and the changing cultural attitudes toward "the singleness-marriage issue." Sees in Mildred Lathbury the prototypic "excellent woman."

52 GUIMARAES, DONA. "The Most Private Eye." *Vogue*, July, pp. 120, 122.
     Review of *A Very Private Eye*. This "comforting book" settles the question of "quintessential Pym. . . . Here is the matrix from which those ten novels emerged." She records here every nuance of her own emotions. She was "a world-class domestic observer."

53 GUNN, H.D. "A Writer Rescued from Oblivion." *Philadelphia Inquirer*, 15 July, p. 3.
     Review of *A Very Private Eye*. Compliments Hazel Holt for the "great authority, intelligence and affection" with which she compiled this collection.

54 HALPERIN, JOHN. "Recent Books on Modern Fiction: British and Irish." *Modern Fiction Studies* 30 (Winter):780-82.
     Review of *A Very Private Eye*. Examines Pym's career and calls her one of the greatest of modern British novelists. "To be able to

draw comfort from the small pleasures and ironies of life . . . may be the greatest gift, beyond her novels, [she] has bequeathed to her readers."

55 HARNETT, LYNN. "Barbara Pym's Diaries and Letters Readable and Revealing." *Portsmouth* (N.H.) *Herald,* 22 July, p. E5.
    Review of *A Very Private Eye.* The memoirs read much like her books. "Her eye for detail—witty, comforting, incongruous, or absurd—is unsurpassed." Finds her eminently rereadable.

56 HEBERLEIN, KATE BROWDER. "Barbara Pym and Anthony Trollope: Communities of Imaginative Participation." *Pacific Coast Philology* 19 (June):95-101.
    Includes portions from 1984.57. Notes that Pym and Trollope share an interest in the clergy, a comic vision, and a celebration of the ordinary; "we can join their communities of imaginative participation and perhaps, like Pym's novelists marquees, create our own."

57 ____. "Communities of Imaginative Participation: The Novels of Barbara Pym." Ph.D. dissertation, University of Washington, 295 pp.
    "Pym's protagonists' curiosity, observation, memory, and ability to adopt another's perspective enrich their isolation and create community." Considers all eleven novels as well as the private papers and discusses the fictional settings that reflect major social changes in England after World War II. Excerpted: 1984.56.

58 HELLER, KAREN. " 'Private Eye': Pym Remains Undercover." *USA Today,* 20 July, p. D3.
    Review of *A Very Private Eye.* Complains that this book is "too little and a bit lazy. It doesn't seem to constitute a life." Wonders whether Pym ever intended her memoirs to be read by the general public.

59 HILDEBRAND, HOLLY. "The Other Side of Pym and Proper Life." *Houston Post,* 22 July, p. F11.
    Review of *A Very Private Eye.* Reveals how she fell in love with Pym's "peculiar kind of magic" after reading *Excellent Women.* Describes her memoirs as "a treasure trove for scholar and simply Pym lover" and Pym as a complex, fascinating, and worldly woman who showed wit and courage in her life.

60 HILL, SUSAN. "Good Books." *Good Housekeeping,* August, p. 153.

Brief review of *A Very Private Eye*. The volume will interest not merely her admirers. Finds here "a likeable, self-deprecating but inwardly tough, very English lady with a sharp eye and a mordant sense of the bizarre and the ridiculous" and a vivid portrait of the past century.

61 HOWE, PAMELA. "The 'Cruelly Perceptive Eye' of a Born Novelist." *Listener* 112 (5 July):14-15.

Only a few writers create a " 'separate', intensely individual and recognisable world, which – once you've entered and felt at home there – subtly alters your vision of the real world and at the same time makes a very agreeable refuge from it." Pym does just that. Reports on her Radio 4 program ("The World of Barbara Pym") as well as on a serial reading for "Story Time" of *Excellent Women* (both in 1984) and a television interview conducted with her at her home in 1977. "Her air of rueful inner amusement and her acute sense of the absurd made her incapable of jabbering away about life and art in the manner of more self-important and unreadable novelists." Comments on her ironic detachment, her religion, her voice, and her life.

62 JARVIS, REV. WILLIAM. "Address Given by the Rev. William Jarvis on the Occasion of the Dedication of a Memorial Plaque and Lectern to Barbara Pym in Finstock Church, Oxford, on the 3rd June 1984, the Sunday after Ascension Day."

Covers a brief history of Finstock, where Pym lived and died. She worshiped in this church; to it she gave her "loyalty and her love." In all of her novels there is a "central value or charm." It is the "noticing of tiny details about people, an amused but kindly probing of their motives and meanings, a tolerance of their hypocrisies and weaknesses, their mental U-turns." Comments on the origin of the title *A Few Green Leaves* and on the final scene between the Rector and Emma Howick. Concludes: "Barbara understood – and God understands – all such hesitant and restless people – maddening, amusing, loveable. The world of Barbara Pym can teach us so much. And we are grateful."

63 KAPP, ISA. "One Woman's Virtue." *Washington Post Book World*, 14 January, p. 3.

Review of *A Very Private Eye*. "In the world of modern fiction, where only sin is guaranteed to spellbind and our prominent authors come most alive in the moments they conjure up death or evil, Pym is a lone sturdy figure, bent on making virtue entertaining."

64 KEMP, PETER. "The Private Barbara Pym." *Listener* 112 (2 August):23-24.

Review of *A Very Private Eye*. Notes many parallels between Pym's life and her fictional concerns in this "fascinating dossier of period minutiae." Like her fiction, her diaries and journals keep "lighting on entertaining oddities." Excerpted: 1986.43.

65 KENDALL, ELAINE. "Bits and Pieces for Posterity." *Los Angeles Times Book Review,* 5 August, pp. 1, 10.

Review of *A Very Private Eye*. Says the collection displays Pym's "resilience, wit and talent" to good advantage. Recommends that it is read slowly, "so the subtle gradation between the sunny and somber extremes are apparent, exactly as Pym's varied and quietly eventful life was lived and savored."

66 KISER, THELMA SCOTT. "New Biographies." *Sunday Independent* (Ashland, Ky.), 17 July, p. 19.

Review of *A Very Private Eye*. Welcomes this as an "intimate introduction" to Pym. Includes biographical details.

67 LARKIN, PHILIP. "Books of the Year." *Observer* (London), 2 December, p. 19.

Cites *A Very Private Eye* as an enhancement to Pym's "still-spiralling" posthumous reputation. Sees here her "dependence on increasingly unsuitable men through a darkening life, only saved by a sunburst of fame at the end in spite of non-publishers." Excerpted: 1986.43.

68 LIDDELL, ROBERT. "Two Friends: Barbara Pym and Ivy Compton-Burnett." *London Magazine,* n.s. 24 (August/September):59-65.

Reminisces about his friendship with Pym from 1933 until her death in 1980. Came to appreciate not only her "original and quaint sense of humour," her passion for English literature, her amusement at "the vagaries of clergy," but also her deeper qualities, including her unselfishness, patience, and endurance. Includes biographical details.

69 LIVELY, PENELOPE. "Barbara Pym: Life as an Art Form." *Sunday Telegraph* (London), 22 July, p. 16.

Review of *A Very Private Eye*. Finds here the evolution and maturation of Pym's style and the accumulation of material over the passing years. Curiously her voice in the novels is "characteristic from the start: to read the first and the last in quick succession is to find little significant change other than a tauter style, a greater economy of expression." Excerpted: 1984.80.

70 ____. "Pyms Aren't What You Thought They Were." *Books & Bookmen,* June, pp. 8-9.

Interviews Hilary Pym, co-editor (with Hazel Holt) of *A Very Private Eye,* who explains why she wanted to publish the papers and comments on the "real Barbara Pym" as revealed in the book. "Barbara's *persona* was very different from that projected on her by her readers." The volume contributes to the reader's perception of the novels' central concern – "gender warfare."

71 LONG, ROBERT EMMET. "Book Reviews." *America* 151 (24 November):348.

Review of *A Very Private Eye.* This book evokes Pym's "own personal qualities as a writer and as a woman. . . . It testifies to Pym's modest yet potent spell." Calls it one of her best books and one that every enthusiast will want to read.

72 LOPEZ, RUTH. "Pym Diaries Show Inspiration for Her Comic World." *Detroit Free Press,* 5 August, p. 27.

Review of *A Very Private Eye.* Pym wrote to "quell her restlessness," and most likely "the gloominess brought on by the way it influenced her to write light comic novels." Her fascination with ordinary people, her passion for learning about those who interested her, her "sharp observations of comic detail and graphic descriptions" – all this is here in the memoirs.

73 McGRATH, REGINA. "A Fine Eye for Life as Literature." *San Francisco Examiner-Chronicle Review,* 19 August, p. 10.

Review of *A Very Private Eye.* Finds extraordinary the way in which "Pym turns daily existence into captivating reading." The reader comes away from this collection feeling that "Pym would have been a great friend to have." The section entitled "The Novelist" offers the "richest" reading; the weakest is the first, covering her years at Oxford.

74 MAHER, BERNARD. "An Excellent Woman?" *Irish Times,* 21 July, p. 13.

Review of *A Very Private Eye.* Finds in Pym's early and middle years a "surprisingly passionate and romantic temperament" that she later "held in check." Like her novels, this book has the quality of "a skilful stitchwork of minutiae and small observations. . . . What nobody can deny [Pym] is the born novelist's gift of making a world of her own, a world which has atmosphere, reality, style."

75 MEADE, MARION. "The Luxury of Summer Reading." *Ms.* 13 (July):21.

Brief review of *A Very Private Eye*. What emerges most vividly from this compilation is Pym's "gloriously wicked sense of humor that makes each of her books an experience to be tasted slowly and savored for a long while afterward."

76 MEYERS, VALERIE. "Recent Books on Modern Fiction: British and Irish." *Modern Fiction Studies* 30 (Winter):783-84.

Reviews Pym's career and life in *A Very Private Eye*. Says that many of the extracts are "trivial and self-conscious." The most interesting material covers the 1930s. Concludes that the book will intrigue only those who know and admire the novels.

77 MILAN, KAREN. "Her Life Also Attained No Fond Return of Love." *Ft. Worth Star-Telegram Books,* 16 September, p. 1.

Review of *A Very Private Eye*. Considers the reasons for Pym's appeal: the "archetypal Pym heroine with her good sense and insight, her limited expectations and ability 'to draw comfort from small pleasure and ironies' and to be splendid under duress; . . . the cosiness of her self-contained world and her eye for comic detail." Finds many parallels between Pym and her heroines. "Only in her relationship with men did she seem to lose control." Says that her comments about her craft are of particular interest to writers.

78 MOOSE, RUTH. "Barbara Pym: The Ordinary Made Special." *Charlotte Observer,* 23 September, p. 15.

Review of *A Very Private Eye*. Finds parallels between Pym and Emily Dickinson. Both wrote of "a small, sharply focused world, intently observed; a paperweight world you peer into like a crystal ball." Calls this compilation *"must* reading" for those who want more of Pym.

79 N[ICHOLS], T[HELMA]. "Fiction." *West Coast Review of Books* 10 (January/February):39.

Brief review of *Some Tame Gazelle*. Finds the characters "witty, intelligent, and often amusing." Pym charms the reader with their "inaction" and reveals "stifled emotions and buried passions." Agrees that she is funnier than Jane Austen.

80 OATES, QUENTIN. "Critics Corner." *Bookseller,* 28 July, pp. 429-30.
    Reviews critical reactions to *A Very Private Eye.* Includes excerpts from 1984.21, 26, 69, 99.

81 PAGE, PATRICIA. "Nonfiction." *San Jose* (Calif.) *Mercury,* 15 August, p. 23.
    Review of *A Very Private Eye.* Surprised to find that Pym, though a spinster, was not one of her "prudent, virginal heroines." Although there are too many gaps here to qualify the book as true autobiography, nevertheless it is "a fascinating self-portrait of an intriguingly reticent and talented woman."

82 PAUL, BARBARA. " 'Very Private Eye' Life of Barbara Pym." *Pittsburgh Press,* 12 August, p. 27.
    Review of *A Very Private Eye.* Like her life, Pym's novels are "quiet and distanced and civilized, a refreshing relief from the ego-wallow" that has dominated much of literature in the 1960s and 1970s. She celebrates the single life as "a means of realizing one's strength."

83 PETERSON, LORNA. "Barbara Pym: A Checklist, 1950-1984." *Bulletin of Bibliography* 41 (December):201-6.
    Lists primary works (arranged chronologically and divided into novels, short stories, and articles) and secondary sources (arranged chronologically and divided into general criticism, reviews, summaries of works, biographical articles, obituaries, and miscellany). "Despite the quality of Barbara Pym's work and the voluminous praise for her witty novels of manners, [she] has not received the scholarly attention she deserves." *See* 1986.10.

84 PEYTON, GEORGE. "Eyes Turned to Pym." *San Diego Union Books,* 22 July, p. 27.
    Review of *A Very Private Eye.* "By its nature this book is jerky and uneven." Finds the last half particularly useful.

85 POOL, GAIL. "Excellent Women." *Nation* 239 (4 August):88-90.
    Review of *A Very Private Eye.* Finds this both painful and rewarding to read. Of particular interest is "Pym's unusual sensibility, which created the peculiar world of her fiction and which we can follow through this selective record." Notes a lack of religious references. Includes biographical details. Excerpted: 1986.43.

86 QUACKENBUSH, RICH. "An Excellent Woman." *Houston Chronicle,* 22 July, p. 19.

Review of *A Very Private Eye*. Calls this memoir "both an absorbing literary record and an engaging portrait of an 'excellent woman' and her time." Includes biographical details.

87 QUIGLEY, ISABEL. "Unprivate Life of 'Prim' Miss Pym." *Tablet*, 25 August, pp. 819-20.

Review of *A Very Private Eye*. Suggests that Pym's literary turnabout may have been due to Pym herself: "a spinster, an Anglican churchwoman, with the personality and looks exactly recognisable as such. . . . No life could have been more consistently invented." In this compilation, Pym seems "amazingly unprivate." Finds "precious little" mention of religion or politics in any deep sense. "And yet, though so much seems breathless, uncritical, self-indulgent and plain silly, there are nuggets of excellence, good observations and a neat sense of comedy." Also finds here great courage in the face of neglect and, later, illness. But the collection lacks the "fuller, richer life-story" that a biographer could show.

88 R., R. "In Print." *Inquiry* 26 (July):32.

Mentions *A Very Private Eye*. Pym now seems to be "coming into her own."

89 REEFER, MARY M. "Barbara Pym Returns with the Same Old Flair." *Kansas City* (Mo.) *Star*, 5 August, p. 19.

Review of *A Very Private Eye*. Says that although Pym lacked "enough spleen in her nature to provide the gossipy diaries of a Virginia Woolf, she did have . . . the searching eye of a camera, with which she recorded the vagaries of the little people she found so interesting." Finds it ironic that the "old-fashioned" quality of her work accounted for her revival.

90 ROWSE, A.L. "My Book of the Year." *Financial Times* (London), 1 December, p. 2.

Cites *A Very Private Eye* because it has "every kind of appeal, biographical and autobiographical" and offers a full portrait of "one of the nicest Oxford women" of his generation. "Quite right: she was the best novelist of her generation."

91 RUBIN, MERLE. "A Very Private Eye." *Christian Science Monitor*, 23 August, pp. 21-22.

Review of *A Very Private Eye*. Like Jane Austen, Pym had "an instinctive wisdom for choosing the kind of personal subjects that by their very limitations gave her talents their greatest scope." In her fiction she has transformed the events of her life into "art of enduring value." The "real" Pym is not in her letters and diaries ("byproducts of life") but in the fiction that she "wove from life."

92 SCHMITZ, EUGENIA. "Nonfiction." *Best Sellers* 44 (September):212.
Review of *A Very Private Eye*. Notes the "buoyant" style and "joy of living and interest in people." The entries' "extreme subjectivity" may bore the reader, however, if read through in one sitting.

93 SEE, CAROLYN. "Plotting Great Escapes for Summer." *Los Angeles Times*, 1 July, p. 9.
Review of *A Very Private Eye*. Recommends this as a vacation between pages: "this brave and remarkable novelist, who barely lived to receive the recognition she deserves."

94 SILVER, ADELE Z. "Barbara Pym – Imprudent Spinster." *Cleveland Plain Dealer*, 22 July, p. 13.
Review of *A Very Private Eye*. This collection answers, in part, the question of how Pym evolved from "the lusty, almost reckless, vibrant, emotional young woman of several unhappy love affairs to the self-contained, middle-aged woman ... without forfeiting her native generosity or becoming embittered." Indicated here, too, is how "hard-won" was her wisdom.

95 SLUNG, MICHAEL. "Oxford, Jumble Sales and Unhappy Love Affairs." *Newsday*, 22 July, pp. 16-17.
Review of *A Very Private Eye*. As in Pym's novels, there was so much unexpected in her life. Notes how odd it is that so much of her characters are "an extension of herself and the world around her." Finds a sadness here, too. "We know, and we don't know, how unhappy and lonely Pym often felt."

96 SMITH, ANNE. "Books: The Pleasures of Reading, 1984." *New Statesman* 108 (December):44.
Names *A Very Private Eye* as "best autobiography."

97 SMITH, LINELL. "A Writer's Growth: Diaries and Letters of Barbara Pym." *Baltimore Sun*, 8 July, p. L8.
Review of *A Very Private Eye*. Finds here the raw material of Pym's art – "quintessential Pym, with slightly more melodrama." But as an autobiography, it is "an unsatisfactory patchwork of whimsical, perhaps perilous, charm."

98 SMITH, WENDY. "Brief Review." *New Republic* 191 (16 July):41.
      Review of *A Very Private Eye*. Although most of Pym's novels are
comedies – "funny, clever, even insightful" – they lack depth. It is a
surprise, therefore, to find in her diaries (reminiscent of Charlotte
Brontë) evidence of a "vibrant, passionate woman who felt things very
deeply and expressed her emotions openly." Calls the diary entries
from her years of rejection "painful" and those from her final days
"deeply moving." Unfortunately, the intervening years are not covered.

99 SPURLING, HILARY. "A Taste of Dust." *Guardian* (Manchester), 29
      July, p. 22.
      Review of *A Very Private Eye*. "The message of this scrappy,
repetitive, often humourless, uneventful and ill-edited book seems to
be that you too – however tame, unadventurous and drab – can be a
novelist." Calls Pym *"an invention."* Excerpted: 1984.80.

100 SWINDEN, PATRICK. *The English Novel of History and Society,*
      1940-1980. London: Macmillan; New York: St. Martin's Press, p. 2.
      Quotes from *Excellent Women* and *Quartet in Autumn* as he
discusses what has happened to the English novel during the
immediate pre- and postwar years. "Too many novels betrayed a sort
of imaginative anaemia and provincialism that was much commented
on by foreign writers and readers."

101 TOEPER, SUSAN. "The Passions of Barbara Pym." *Daily News* (New
      York), 29 July, pp. 13-14.
      Review of *A Very Private Eye*. Finds in these "wonderful nuggets
of self-advice . . . and revealing jottings . . . a new Pym, a different Pym,
and one that is every bit as endearing as her remarkable novels."
Includes an introduction to her ten novels with brief plot summaries
and commentaries on characterization, themes, and humor.

102 TYLER, ANNE. Foreword to *Excellent Women, Jane and Prudence,*
      and *An Unsuitable Attachment*. New York: Quality Paperback Book
      Club, pp. v-xviii.
      Finds in these three volumes all of Pym's favorite themes: "an
enduring respect for the modest, so-called trivial details of life; a rueful
amusement at the silliness between the sexes; and more than a hint
that women – especially sensible, virtuous, independent women – are in
many ways far stronger than men can ever hope to be, although the
women wouldn't dream of letting them find that out." Examines
possible similarities between Pym and Jane Austen. Comments briefly
on her other seven novels.

103 WAUGH, AUBERON. "That's Romance with a Rotter!" *Daily Mail* (London), 19 July, p. 7.
   Review of *A Very Private Eye*. Notes Pym's "novelist's eye and a sweetness of nature which bordered on the eccentric." This book celebrates the "triumph of niceness" of modern-day horrors and will increase one's understanding and enjoyment of the novels.

104 WIDMAYER, RICHARD A. "Nonfiction." *Rocky Mountain Review of Language and Literature* 39 (1):77-79.
   Brief review of *A Very Private Eye*.

105 WILCE, GILLIAN. "Borderland." *New Statesman* 108 (24 August):23.
   Review of *A Very Private Eye*. Finds of value the "glimpses of the commerce" between the private Pym and the writer Pym. "The book has the momentum of the private life," and yet always there is the detachment of the writer. Finds that Pym "turns a private, sardonic and unsentimental eye on the detail of her own life."

106 WILSON, A.N. "Sock for Posterity." *Literary Review* 83 (September):4-6.
   Review of *A Very Private Eye*. While doubting the worth of this volume, expresses gratitude to the editors for revealing "the number of dead-ends, false trails and cul-de-sacs which as a novelist Pym could have turned down." Here we see Pym "mapping out her world." Hers is a consoling voice. While some of these experiences might have pleased many twentieth-century publishers, "it was not perfect material for her sort of fiction."

107 WYATT, LOUISE. "A Detailed View of Barbara Pym's Life in Her Own Words." *Free Press* (London), 17 August, p. 13.
   Review of *A Very Private Eye*. This collection reminds the reader that Pym's novels are distinctive in their "quality, validity and flavor." Her spirituality is embodied in her art, her life's work.

108 WYMARD, ELEANOR B. "Secular Faith of Barbara Pym." *Commonweal*, 110 (13 January):19-21.
   Finds it unfortunate that Pym's first ten novels are "embraced . . . as well-crafted entertainments when, indeed, they share affinities with the existentialist mood of modern fiction." Although her world is at first "strangely insular" and Pym's essential questions are "disguised by the tone of high comedy," ultimately her characters "neither escape nor endure their experience. Rather, they become more human by trying to live with it, affirming their lot in private ritualized gestures or

formal ceremonies." Thus her central theme is "the incommunicable uniqueness of each ordinary person."

109 ZELENKO, BARBARA. "Nonfiction." *Library Journal* 109 (15 May):1126.
    Brief review of *A Very Private Eye.* "Feminists and students of Pym's work as well as her many fans should have a field day with this fascinating book." She is an "astute observer of human foibles."

1985

1 ADAMS, PHOEBE-LOU. "Brief Reviews." *Atlantic* 255 (June):104.
    Brief review of *Crampton Hodnet.* Pym was right to leave this novel unpublished because it was too dated. "It is quite madly nineteen-thirtyish, but admirers of Pym's work will nevertheless enjoy it."

2 ANON. "Briefly Noted: Fiction." *New Yorker* 61 (29 July):76-77.
    Brief review of *Crampton Hodnet.* "Readers will not be dismayed by anything but Barbara Pym's doubts."

3 ANON. *"Crampton Hodnet* by Barbara Pym." *Book-of-the-Month Club News,* 1 September, p. 15.
    Review of *Crampton Hodnet.* This new novel is a cause for Pym fans to celebrate. Calls the novel "vintage Pym – a wryly elegant comedy of manners." Pym observes her characters from the inside and makes them "figures of dignity as well as fun."

4 ANON. "Fiction." *Kirkus Reviews* 53 (1 May):389-90.
    Review of *Crampton Hodnet.* "A funny and fast-moving book [that] will delight Pym lovers as well as provide an enlightening introduction" for those unfamiliar with her work. The book's datedness provides much of its "charm."

5 ANON. "Fiction." *Publishers Weekly* 227 (19 April):69.
    Review of *Crampton Hodnet.* In spite of this novel's "slight" plot, the "sharp" characterizations and the "brilliant" dialogue make this a "very funny novel [which] can stand on its own as entertaining fare." Enunciated here is a theme that Pym probes "more searchingly" in her later works – "the difficulties of reconciling romantic fantasy with the reality of life." Excerpted: 1986.43.

6 ANON. "Holiday Reading: Fiction." *Observer* (London), 21 July, p. 22.
    Cites *Crampton Hodnet*. "The familiar North Oxford cast of spinsters and curates, but playing it all for laughs."

7 ANON. "Nonfiction." *Washington Post Book World,* 30 June, p. 12.
    Brief review of *A Very Private Eye*. Finds many "riches" contained in this "intimate memorial" to Pym.

8 BAILEY, HILARY. "Versions of Irony." *Guardian* (Manchester), 14 July, p. 9.
    Brief review of *Crampton Hodnet*. Finds the book "fairly baffling, though skilfully done." The "only conscious" character in the book is Jessie Morrow.

9 BAILEY, PAUL. "Period Hoot." *Observer* (London), 30 June, p. 23.
    Review of *Crampton Hodnet*. Calls this "extraordinarily assured" novel a "performance" and very funny, almost a parody of the later books. Buried beneath her "jauntiness" is a certain cynicism as she accounts for the relationship between Barbara Bird and Francis Cleveland. Concludes that Pym is now being "overpraised." Comparisons with Jane Austen are not warranted, for Pym's understanding of the human heart never reached the depth displayed in *Persuasion*. Excerpted: 1986.43.

10 BATCHELOR, JUDY L. "Not-Quite-Indexers in Fiction (and Non-Fiction)." *Indexer* 14 (October):277.
    Refers to *Jane and Prudence* (in which Jane plunges dishes and glasses "indiscriminately into the water without any attempt at a scientific arrangement or classification") and *Quartet in Autumn* (in which Marcia "in the early stages of her loneliness . . . arranges the tins in her store cupboard"). Both examples fall under the heading of "not-quite-indexers."

11 BECKER, ALIDA. "Fiction." *San Jose* (Calif.) *Mercury News,* 12 May, p. 12.
    Review of *Crampton Hodnet*. This novel's "edges are sharper, its messages less subtle, its plotting more forced" than the later works, but it does have a "bittersweet charm." The novel makes "an intriguing prelude to the more complex and finely drawn investigations that were to come."

12 B[ELL], H[AZEL] K. "The Image of the Indexer?" *Indexer* 14 (April):202.

Discusses the overall image of the indexer in fiction and the "distinctly patronizing" attitude to indexers in Pym's novels. Notes that "the stock image of indexers is to be docile, eccentric, absurd, well out of the centre of life's stream."

13 _____. "'Thankless Task' Accomplished for Pym." *Indexer* 14 (April):189.

Review of *A Very Private Eye*. Comments on the book's index: "originality and charm, showing respect and devotion for its text; wholly appropriate for the author who gave us Mildred Lathbury and Dulcie Mainwaring, and wrote so warmly and wittily of our 'thankless task.'"

14 BROOKNER, ANITA. "The Loneliness of Miss Pym." *Sunday Times* (London), 23 June, p. 11.

Review of *Crampton Hodnet*. Comparisons between Pym and Jane Austen are "careless" and "probably false." Pym's tone is "limpid rather than incisive," her story-telling is "bland," and her characters are meek. Calls this sprightly novel a "celebration" of Pym's innocence.

15 B[ROSNAHAN], J[OHN]. "Adult Fiction." *Booklist,* 1 April, p. 1082.

Review of *Crampton Hodnet*. Calls this "vintage Pym," filled with prototypes of characters, situations, and settings that she would develop in later novels. Finds interesting the intersection of academic and ecclesiastical circles.

16 DANIEL, MARGARET. "Early Pym." *Church Times* (London), 26 July, p. 6.

Brief review of *Crampton Hodnet*. Although this novel is "less subtle" than the later ones and the "gentility is dated," the characters are familiar – especially Miss Morrow, who looks forward to Pym's later excellent women. "Comic moments abound, and the humour is less complicated by those tendrils of stoicism that entwine her maturer comedy."

17 DIGILIO, ALICE. "Teatime at Oxford." *Washington Post Book World,* 9 June, p. 9.

Review of *Crampton Hodnet*. Pym's wryly self-deprecatory tone holds together this "timeless" novel. If there is a weakness, it is that Pym seems uncertain "whose consciousness would anchor the novel." Excerpted: 1986.43.

18 DORRIS, MICHAEL. "In Short: Fiction." *New York Times Book Review,* 1 September, p. 14.

Review of *Crampton Hodnet.* Identifies Pym's understanding, compassion, and precise language – all of which make "compelling" the "constricted" action. The novel's humor, insights, and small surprises contain "a freshness that is irresistible."

19 DRABBLE, MARGARET, ed. "Barbara Mary Crampton Pym (1913-1980)." In *The Oxford Companion to English Literature.* 5th ed. Oxford and New York: Oxford University Press, p. 801.

Brief biographical entry. Calls her novels "satirical tragic-comedies of middle-class life [that] contain some distinctive portraits of church-going spinsters and charismatic priests; many of the relationships described consist of a kind of celibate flirtation."

20 DUFFY, MARTHA. "Blue Velvet." *Time* 125 (24 June):81.

Review of *Crampton Hodnet.* Comments on the secret of Pym's success: "her reliability." Finds charming here "the glimpse it offers of Pym's imagination as it pauses for a moment in perfect understanding of a character. That sympathy stresses beyond the horizon of comedy." Mentions *Jane and Prudence.*

21 DUTKA, J. "Books." *Canadian Catholic Review,* April, pp. 33-34.

Review of *A Very Private Eye.* Says that this volume is "required reading" for all those who love her novels. Conveyed here is Pym's difficult life as a writer, her near-bitterness, and her self-doubt. But she could laugh at herself. Her journals "suggest that she cultivated emotion in order to examine it with a novelist's analytical eye." Ranks Pym as "one of the most artistically and humanly satisfying of recent novelists."

22 DYER, RICHARD. "Brimming with Pymlichkeit." *Boston Globe,* 14 May, p. 72.

Review of *Crampton Hodnet.* "The book is fresh, funny, a bit unfinished in detail, and, obviously, already brimming over with *Pymlichkeit.*" Finds new in this novel the North Oxford ambience.

23 FENTON, JAMES. "A Team of Those Old Oxford Blues." *Times* (London), 20 June, p. 11.

Review of *Crampton Hodnet.* Although this novel is "more broadly comic" than some of Pym's others, finds here "a lurking cynicism, a pervasive sense of disappointment in life." Comments on Pym's lack of values, perceiving instead "only projected fears and eagerly awaited disappointments. She is obsessed with surfaces, with fabrics and foibles." The novel will not give the reader much comfort. "It is too unsatisfactory."

24 FULLER, EDMUND. "High Farce in North Oxford." *Wall Street Journal,* 28 May, p. 28.

Review of *Crampton Hodnet.* Much of this book is "as good" as anything Pym ever wrote. "It is an unmalicious tale of infatuations and follies in young and old within the formal precincts of Oxford, which is seen less as a seat of learning than as an inbred community of self-absorbed, mildly eccentric people."

25 GARDAM, JANE. "Kimp Lovers." *Books & Bookmen,* June, p. 29.

Review of *Crampton Hodnet.* In spite of this novel's "care-free" construction and missing "intricacies and nuances" of her later work, the voice here is Pym's, "her eyes and ears never sharper and her dialogue ... is better than it ever is again." It is also her "funniest" book. Sometimes serious themes are "disguised as jokes."

26 GILMAN, JAYNE. "A Long-Lost Oxford Novel Brings the 30's Back to Life." *Oxford Mail,* 2 July, p. 8.

Review of *Crampton Hodnet.* "Admirers of Miss Pym's later novels have an unexpected treat in store." Pym knew her world of North Oxford in the 1930s "intimately."

27 GOLDSTEIN, WILLIAM. "A Novel, a Biography, a Play: A Peek inside the Pym Estate." *Publishers Weekly* 228 (4 October):43.

Interview with Hazel Holt. Mentions *Crampton Hodnet, An Academic Question* (tentatively titled *The Scholar's Wife*), a collection of letters, and other projects.

28 HALIO, JAY L. "Fiction and Reality." *Southern Review* 21 (Winter):210.

Review of *No Fond Return of Love.* This "pleasantly amusing" novel strains credibility. "Life is not that neatly arranged." The writing lacks Jane Austen's "depth and fine wit."

29 HAMILTON-SMITH, BARBARA. "Savouring Pym's Number Two." *Catholic Herald,* 23 August, p. 15.

Review of *Crampton Hodnet.* Comments on the characters ("general disillusion with men" and women as "victims or tormentors"), the setting ("a pre-Betjeman horror of Victoriana"), and parallels with E.F. Benson and Rose Macaulay. Wonders ("with a mixture of horror and delight") how Pym might have written this had she been in a suburban Catholic parish.

30 HASTINGS, SELINA. "Recent Fiction." *Daily Telegraph* (London), 21 June, p. 13.
     Review of *Crampton Hodnet*. As a period piece, finds this novel charming and "sharply funny." Its world is "reassuringly recognisable" with a familiar cast of characters.

31 HEBERLEIN, KATE BROWDER. "Barbara Pym." *Contemporary Literature* 25 (Fall):368-71.
     Review of *A Very Private Eye*. Calls this collection a disappointment to anyone expecting an autobiography. Notes the omission of much archival material. Disproportionate attention is paid to her early years before she began to publish novels. The relationship between her life and novels is unclear. Explanations of her love life (did she have a sex life?) and her friendships need more development. The collection leaves the reader "with a vague and misleading impression of her personal life and little understanding of how she transmuted her odd, quiet, rather sad life into her odd, quietly comic fiction."

32 HENDERSON, HEATHER. "Vain Affairs of the Heart." *MacLean's* 98 (24 June):62.
     Review of *Crampton Hodnet*. "Pym is a quiet subversive, deliberately confining her art to a small canvas. She has a rare gift for observing small details that speak volumes. . . . [This novel] will only add to her reputation as an elegant satirist."

33 HILL, ROSEMARY. "Consoling Humour." *Country Life,* 8 August, p. 12.
     Review of *Crampton Hodnet*. Says that Pym is at her "funniest and bitterest." To those readers "whose fears are loneliness, personal failure and turning up in the wrong clothes, [this novel] will indeed bring some comfort and much delight."

34 HUDSON, CHRISTOPHER. "Pym's with Zing." *Standard* (London), 19 June, p. 11.
     Review of *Crampton Hodnet*. Finds here all the "ingredients" that readers of Pym look for: "the sharp eye for idiosyncrasies; the comedy of gentle souls resorting to desperate strategems to avoid morally compromising situations." But with the exception of Miss

Doggett and Miss Morrow (whose relationship is "a delight"), the characters suffer from "a sporadic, incomplete existence on the page."

35 INGRAMS, RICHARD. "Books of the Year." *Spectator* 255 (7 December):37.

Cites *Crampton Hodnet* as containing "a number of very good jokes."

36 IYER, PICO. "Tricks of Self-Consciousness." *Partisan Review* 52 (Summer):286.

Review of *No Fond Return of Love.* "Pym is determined to have almost no designs upon the reader, no great expectations, no intricate patterns in her plot. Her charm lies in her innocence of literary fashion, her willingness to sew together a series of shrewd observations into nothing more, nor less, than a solid, old-fashioned entertainment." Excerpted: 1986.43.

37 KAUFMAN, JAMES. "Now in Paper." *Christian Science Monitor Book Review,* 2 August, p. 7.

Brief review of *A Very Private Eye.* Reveals Pym as both "interesting and not exactly as you would imagine." Her novels are "an acquired taste."

38 KEENER, FREDERICK M. "Barbara Pym Herself and Jane Austen." *Twentieth Century Literature* 31 (Spring):89-110.

Considers Pym's first ten novels and tests the usefulness of comparing her to Jane Austen. But keeps the question of debts in perspective, for they are "not by any means the whole story." Includes biographical details.

39 KEMP, PETER. "Oxford Beginnings." *Listener* 113 (27 June):31.

Review of *Crampton Hodnet.* Finds here all the qualities that give Pym's novels their appeal: "a connoisseur's eye for the absurd, almost disconcerting candor, the ability to note shortcomings with amused equanimity, placidly sombre insights into life's graver aspects." In Jessie Morrow, Pym "envisages what she was likely to become." In Barbara Bird, she reflects on her Oxford days. Most "distinctive and distinguished" of all is Pym's ability to "combine chilling moments . . . with the enthralling oddities she rummages out from even the most ordinary-looking lives."

40 KENDALL, ELAINE. "Fiction." *Los Angeles Times,* 23 July, p. B4.

Brief review of *Crampton Hodnet.*

41 ____. "New Fiction." *Los Angeles Times,* 4 August, p. 8.
Brief review of *Crampton Hodnet.*

42 KING, FRANCIS. "Frequent Smiles at Pym's No. 1." *Spectator* 254 (29 June):28.
Review of *Crampton Hodnet.* Confesses that the novel made him smile "frequently at the delicate, teasing artistry of scene after scene." The "key" to the novel lies in the fact that Mr. Latimer and Miss Morrow along with Francis Cleveland and Barbara Bird "find themselves the victims of constant observation and comment." But the novel is "uncomfortably artificial" because of the many coincidences that enable other characters to "keep tabs" on these couples. Says that the novel evokes memories of Ivy Compton-Burnett. This novel "eerily evokes a vanished world ... of people too small to contain the emotions that seem to overwhelm them, of sensibility constantly being held in check by sense, and a rueful, resigned acceptance of the trivial and humdrum. Under all the rattle of the fun, there is always a plangent note of sadness."

43 LIVELY, PENELOPE. "Deep in the Pym Country." *Sunday Telegraph* (London), 30 June, p. 10.
Review of *Crampton Hodnet.* Calls it "extraordinary" that this first novel is "very good – less polished, indeed, than the rest, occasionally clumsy, somewhat slapdash where narrative is concerned – but full of delights and conspicuously part of the oeuvre." Comments on its tone ("dry, wry, ironic"), setting (North Oxford), central concern (love), and characterization.

44 LONG, ROBERT EMMET. "Fiction." *America* 153 (2 November):285-86.
Review of *Crampton Hodnet.* "It is Pym in splendid form – livelier and gayer than that of her later novels, but with a loss of innocence." As in Austen's novels, finds here "a classically shaped study of personal relationships in the English provinces."

45 LUCY, MARGARET. "Whispers of Wit but Unlucky in Love." *Catholic Herald,* 15 March, p. 8.
Review of *A Very Private Eye.* Pym is "boldness itself" in her letters and personality. Pym is "witty but never cruel, perceptive and kindly, enjoying everything that comes her way and fighting cancer without self-pity." On finishing this "charming" book, readers must feel that they have lost a friend.

46 McCLURG, JOCELYN. "Posthumous Pym: Less Than Culture." *Hartford* (Conn.) *Courant,* 22 September, p. G3.

Review of *Crampton Hodnet.* Complains of its weakness in structure and plot.

47 McGURN, WILLIAM. "Book Reviews." *American Spectator* 18 (November):46.

Review of *Crampton Hodnet.* Although the novel is a bit overwritten and the characters are "somewhat raw," this is probably her funniest. Pym tells the story with "a keen sense of human foibles, muted by the English penchant for understanding." The book never degenerates into contempt for fellow humans.

48 MARSH, PAMELA. "Early Pym Unsettling, Comforting." *Christian Science Monitor,* 7 June, p. B2.

Review of *Crampton Hodnet.* Discusses Pym's "brilliant ... yet somehow vaguely comforting" irony. Pym entertains the reader with her favorite subject, love—"between the sexes, but love almost devoid of sex."

49 MURPHY, MARESE. "Life Work." *Irish Times,* 29 June, p. 10.

Review of *Crampton Hodnet.* Finds not a wasted word in this "devastating study" of life in Oxford. Her humor is "at its sharpest" and her characters are observed with "a succinct perceptiveness" reminiscent of E.F. Benson.

50 NARDIN, JANE. *Barbara Pym.* Twayne's English Authors Series, no. 406. Boston: Twayne, 154 pp.

Introductory study of Pym's life and career, noting the origins and development of themes, character types, and style. Includes chronology, notes, bibliography (listing primary and secondary sources), and index.

51 NEWMAN, JULIE. "Novel of the Month." *Words,* August, pp. 57-59.

Review of *Crampton Hodnet.* This novel bears out Pym's reputation as "a wickedly funny satirist of the myths of romantic love." But she shows no contempt for the "real thing" and is in "no sense a man-hater." In the author's world, "pain is not everlasting, spinsters are not necessarily benighted, nor is marriage automatically the fulfillment of a woman's every desire." Readers of *Jane and Prudence* will have to revise their expectations. "Far from creating a cosy self-contained world, Pym narrows her focus only to put human foibles under a stronger lens, so that they appear in sharper relief." Includes a review of Pym's evolving career.

52 PHELAN, NANCY. "Early Pym and a Late Wesley." *Sydney Morning Herald,* 19 October, p. 28.

Review of *Crampton Hodnet.* Comments on Pym's considerable achievement as a humorist; her "quiet, almost sly, very delicate satire . . . misses nothing yet is never unkind." Although this book lacks "the poignancy and subtlety" of her later novels, it is immediately recognizable as a Pym novel.

53 PHILIP, NEIL. "Final Accolade." *Times Educational Supplement* (London), 5 April, p. 37.

Review of *A Very Private Eye.* The most interesting section describes Pym trying to come to terms with rejection after success. Notes that the book is "dull with a sought and welcomed dullness that is the foundation of [her] ethic, which is that the trivial concerns of mundane lives are important." The editing is "haphazard and unhelpful."

54 PORTER, DOROTHY. "Cause for Laughter in the Bodleian." *Glasgow Herald,* 22 June, p. 17.

Review of *Crampton Hodnet.* Comments on Pym's "impeccable" control of idiom and tone and scenes that make the reader laugh aloud. Although set in the Oxford of the late 1930s, the novel is not dated. As an invented village, Crampton Hodnet "becomes a motif for all the deceptions that form the fabric of daily life."

55 QUIGLEY, ISABEL. "Period Piece." *Tablet,* 10 August, p. 64.

Review of *Crampton Hodnet.* Notices here the "fly-in-amber quality of the Pym diaries: the daily dullness, the melancholy, put across with amusing exactness." Finds encapsulated here almost everything found in her other novels: "a small community involved with church (High Anglican) and academic life: curates and dons, spinsters of both sexes, gossip and malice, sex and frustration, hopelessly inadequate and useless men, lonely, more sympathetic women." Comments on parallels between Pym and Miss Morrow.

56 RADNER, SANFORD. "Barbara Pym's People." *Western Humanities Review* 39 (Summer):172-77.

Seeks to define Pym as both comic writer and social critic. Finds in her first ten novels a central theme. As adults come together, they unconsciously play out a fantasy – "a self-denying mother indulges her narcissistic little boy."

57 ROSSEN, JANICE. "Love in the Great Libraries: Oxford in the Work of Barbara Pym." *Journal of Modern Literature* 12 (July):277-96.

Examines the influence of Oxford on Pym's novels and unpublished works. Four novels especially carry the theme of the relationship between love and work stemming from the university: *Some Tame Gazelle, Crampton Hodnet, Jane and Prudence,* and *No Fond Return of Love.* "In the sense that she wrote intensely about Oxford feelings, relationships, and attitudes, she did write the Oxford novel she longed to write."

58 RYAN, ALAN. "Fiction." *Cleveland Plain Dealer,* 9 June, p. 22.

Review of *Crampton Hodnet.* Praises this "immensely engaging" book for its "meticulous writing, penetrating observation of human nature, sly and sparkling dialogue, a warm pleasure in both the frailties and the strengths of the human heart, a marvelous sense of humor tempered by understanding," and an "almost Dickensian gallery" of characters.

59 SADLER, LYNN VEACH. "Spinsters, Non-Spinsters, and Men in the World of Barbara Pym." *Critique* 26 (Spring):141-54.

Reassesses Pym's attitudes toward spinsters, nonspinsters, and men in the first ten novels. Although largely a prefeminist who finds fault on both sides of the battle between the sexes, "Pym is aware of the traditional limitations society imposes on women." Both men and women come in for their share of "genial ridicule and humor. . . . In the Pym world, bores and boors can be male and female, and men can out-spinster spinsters." If there are indeed many spinsters in her fictional world, "she makes us believe, without suspicion of her miscalculation, that the reason is simple: here is England as it really is."

60 SCHOFIELD, MARY ANNE. "Well-Fed or Well-Loved? – Patterns of Cooking and Eating in the Novels of Barbara Pym." *University of Windsor Review* 18 (Spring/Summer):1-8.

Examines culinary rituals as thematic center in *Some Tame Gazelle* through *An Unsuitable Attachment.* Notes parallels between a focus on food and eating in Pym's novels and anthropological interests in Levi-Strauss's *The Raw and the Cooked, Introduction to a Science of Mythology.* Concludes that Pym's novels become "almost anthropological studies of the civilizing process of man, his eating habits, and the culturing powers of certain foods." She underscores "the isolation and hunger that twentieth-century men and women continually face."

61 SEYMOUR, MIRANDA. "Spinsters in Their Prime." *Times Literary Supplement,* 28 June, p. 720.

Review of *Crampton Hodnet.* Finds here an "excessive eagerness to establish the looks, habits and clothes of each character as soon as his or her name is introduced." In spite of the inappropriate title, thin plot, and repeated jokes, Pym's clear intelligence, high spirits, satirical eye, and "sharply funny" handling of dialogue contribute to this novel's readability. It is the most "irresistibly cheerful" of Pym's novels.

62 SEYMOUR-SMITH, MARTIN. "Cambridge Blue Stocking and Northern Grit." *Financial Times* (London), 22 June, p. 22.

Brief review of *Crampton Hodnet.* "It is a delightful although limited comedy . . . not her shrewdest or most deeply felt work, but very well worth while issuing now."

63 SLACKMAN, MICHAEL. "The Annual *Biography* Evaluative Survey." *Biography* 8 (Fall):288.

Brief review of *A Very Private Eye.* Calls this an "uneven" book, stronger in the latter parts.

64 SPICE, NICHOLAS. "Costa del Pym." *London Review of Books,* 4 July, p. 10.

Review of *Crampton Hodnet.* This novel argues for "acceptance over rebellion, limitation over release, loss-cutting over risk-taking, and resignation over hope." Discusses the three love affairs that develop and dwindle, reducing "the universe of love to a narrow and shallow place." Finds the novel's title to be "eccentric, mildly enigmatic and brilliantly apt."

65 STETZ, MARGARET DIANE. "*Quartet in Autumn:* New Light on Barbara Pym as a Modernist." *Arizona Quarterly* 41 (Spring):24-37.

Dismisses the idea that Pym's books are "just like" Jane Austen's and links the narrative devices in *Quartet in Autumn* to Virginia Woolf's *Mrs. Dalloway.* What matters in both novels is "consciousness itself." Pym conveys her character's consciousness using the methods of a modernist: "simultaneity, association, imagery, memory, and dreams." For Pym, Woolf, and other great modernists, "the inner life in motion is the true source of both coherence and beauty in fiction."

66 STEWART, J.I.M. *The Naylors*. London: Victor Gollancz, p. 87.

So familiar and distinctive is Pym's imagined world that the narrator in *The Naylors* complains, "Encounters like that . . . make me feel like a character in Barbara Pym. Perhaps that's what I am: *anima naturaliter Pym.*"

67 STUEWE, PAUL. "Fiction." *Quill and Quire* 51 (August):49.

Review of *Crampton Hodnet*. "The novel's hilarious variations on the comic possibilities of courtship are worked out with rigour as well as vigour." Anyone who appreciates Pym's "special brand of wry but compassionate humour" will enjoy this book.

68 SUTTON, JUDITH. "Fiction." *Library Journal* 110 (1 May):80.

Review of *Crampton Hodnet*. Finds evident here Pym's "youth and inexperience." Some sections of the book are overwritten, but it is "both interesting as a look into Pym's early work and amusing in its own right."

69 NO ENTRY.

70 TOEPPER, SUSAN. "A Perfect, Posthumous Pym." *Daily News* (New York), 26 May, p. 33.

Review of *Crampton Hodnet*. Calls this "a sly, vicious, mischievous farce." The courtship scenes are "Pym at her wildest."

71 TOMPKINS, PAT. "Fiction." *San Francisco Examiner,* 28 April, p. 14.

Review of *Crampton Hodnet*. This is among Pym's funniest novels. Although it lacks the subtlety of her "more mature" novels, "it needn't be excused as a first novel; its youthful high spirits are part of its charm."

72 TREASE, GEOFFREY. "New Fiction." *British Book News,* September, p. 555.

Review of *Crampton Hodnet*. Finds interesting the character types that recur in later fiction. "Dim people and dusty settings always made [Pym's] wit scintillate by contrast, and never more brightly than here." The author gets "much fun" out of her tiny dramas.

73 WILCE, GILLIAN. "Crampton Hodnet." *New Statesman* 110 (5 July):30.

Review of *Crampton Hodnet*. "The novel is sprightly in much the same fashion as the persona of . . . Pym's younger diaries and deftly organised. . . . But its early indications of a talent to amuse are primarily for what the introduction calls 'faithful readers of the novels.' "

74 WILSON, A.N. "Daffodil Yellow and Coral Pink." *Literary Review* 84 (June):43-44.

    Review of *Crampton Hodnet*. From the start of her career, Pym's world was "finished and fashioned." Discusses the novel's two interwoven plots and period details, Pym's humor ("delicious smiles"), her views on marriage and the relations between the sexes (handled with "relentless glibness").

75 WYATT, WOODROW. "Chapter III: Paradise in Oxford." In *Confessions of an Optimist*, London: Collins, p. 71.

    While browsing in a Madison Avenue bookshop, he came upon Pym's diaries and realized that he knew her quite well. "How dim of me to lose so great a heroine from my memory: I must have been too preoccupied with myself to recognize genius when I met it."

1986

1 ANON. "Fiction." *Kirkus Reviews* 54 (1 July):968-69.

    Review of *An Academic Question*. Calls this a minor but intriguing novel, "studded with luminescent thumbnail characterizations and, on occasion, deliciously funny" scenes.

2 ANON. "New in Paperback: Fiction." *Washington Post Book World,* 22 June, p. 12.

    Review of *Some Tame Gazelle*. "There is little drama, but there is a succession of amusing day-to-day occurrences which make one smile, chuckle, and nod one's head that, yes, all is vanity." Calls this the "perfect introduction" to Pym.

3 ANON. "New in Paperback: Fiction." *Washington Post Book World,* 26 October, p. 12.

    Review of *An Unsuitable Attachment, Quartet in Autumn,* and *A Few Green Leaves*. These three novels give a span of Pym, from early comedy of manners to *Quartet,* "when the trendy modern world had begun to intrude on the self-containment and circumscribed lives of her characters."

4 ARDENER, EDWIN. "My Friend Miss Pym." *Sunday Telegraph* (London), 6 July, p. 14.

Reminisces about his friendship with Pym from 1948 to 1962 and later. Recounts their first meeting at the International African Institute and subsequent visits. Comments on *Some Tame Gazelle, Excellent Women,* and "Across a Crowded Room," notes the anthropological references in her work, and says that the "post-exilic" Pym is tougher. Two features give "a peculiar frisson" to her novels: the "quiet detective-like tracking" and that "strange unreliability" that certain characters show. "As far as we were concerned at the time, she was not a major novelist. And now she's dead, experts on Barbara Pym are appearing who know more about her than she knew herself." *See* 1986.15.

5 B., H.H. "Early Pym Forecasts Later Work." *Anniston Star,* 9 June, p. 17.

Calls *Crampton Hodnet* "a pleasant dress rehearsal" for later novels.

6 BAILEY, JOHN. "Ladies." *London Review of Books,* 4 September, pp. 10-11.

Review of *An Academic Question.* Finds this novel "as readable and characteristic" as any by Pym. "[It] has a proper triviality, an exact lightness of touch, which keeps up the reader's curiosity without his noticing there is any plot at all." Considers her humor, her "moral reflexes," and says that like Jane Austen, "Pym can be read as either optimist or pessimist, cheerful do-gooder or secret and bitter misanthrope." Also discusses similarities and differences between Pym and Anita Brookner's *A Misalliance* and refers to *Crampton Hodnet, Quartet in Autumn, An Unsuitable Attachment, Less Than Angels, The Sweet Dove Died,* and *A Very Private Eye.*

7 BARR, CHARLES. "The 'Miracle' of Rediscovery." *Listener* 116 (31 June):24.

Review of *An Academic Question.* To publish this novel does "disservice" to Pym. In heroine and genre, she was moving "consciously outside" her territory and was displeased with the result. Readers are likely to share that response. And yet the novel is fascinating for its "sourcebook quality" and its status as a "failed experiment."

8 B[ELL], H[AZEL] K. "A Pymian Occasion." *Indexer* 15 (October):66.

Reviews a Barbara Pym conference held at St. Hilda's College, Oxford, 4-5 July. "It is given to few of our trade to have conferences held in their honour; but this one was as truly deserved as it was thoroughly enjoyed – despite the pervasive sense of being most drily observed from above." Brief reference to *An Academic Question.*

9 BENET, DIANA. *Something to Love: Barbara Pym's Novels.* Columbia: University of Missouri Press, 144 pp.

Examines the novelist as "a chronicler of universal problems" whose focus – the many guises of love – moves, shapes, or disfigures all of her major characters. When romantic love fails them or is not an option, the characters seek sustenance in the affections of friendship or family ties, in the Christian love of neighbor, in " 'child substitutes' human or animal, or in the asexual 'unsentimental tenderness . . . expressed in small gestures of solicitude' that one solitary soul might extend to another." Covers *Some Tame Gazelle* through *An Unsuitable Attachment.*

10 BERNDT, JUDY. "Barbara Pym: A Supplementary List of Secondary Sources." *Bulletin of Bibliography* 43 (June):76-80.

Supplements Lorna Peterson's bibliography (*see* 1984.83). Lists secondary sources chronologically and divided into general criticism, reviews, bibliographical articles, obituaries, and miscellany.

11 BLAIR, ALISON. "Style: Who Has It and Who Doesn't." *Gentleman's Quarterly* 56 (January):104.

After the Museum of Modern Art, lists Pym as someone who has style.

12 BRACE, KEITH. "The Lasting Taste of Pym." *Birmingham Post,* 14 August, p. 10.

Review of *An Academic Question.* This novel reveals Pym's unfamiliarity with "the remote, edgy newer universities." Although there is the expected humor, the novel is "thin." *Crampton Hodnet,* on the other hand, is "a quite brilliant comedy of manners, one of her finest books, funny, atmospheric."

13 BROOKNER, ANITA. "The Bitter Fruits of Rejection." *Spectator 257* (19 July): 30-31.

General appraisal of Pym with reference to Robert Emmet Long's *Barbara Pym* (*see* 1986.39). The diaries revealed that Pym was "a mass of contradictions, the sort of woman whose persona strikes most continentals as baffling, yet harbouring a bitterness, a tragic wistfulness, and even a touch of mania or obsessiveness." She transferred her preoccupations directly to the novels. Finds her reputation puzzling. Responded to: 1986.36.

14 BYATT, A.S. "Marginal Lives." *Times Literary Supplement,* 8 August, p. 862.

Review of *An Academic Question.* Pym's attempt to write a "sharp," "swinging" novel was a mistake; the result is "thin and unappealing." Wonders why her novels have attracted academic interest.

15 CAMPBELL, JENNY. "Jenny Campbell Joins the Barbara Pym Groupies." *Sunday Times* (London), 27 July, p. 44.

Reports on a conference – "Barbara Pym: Her Life and Work" – held at St. Hilda's College, Oxford, to coincide with the publication of *An Academic Question.* Comments on the growing "Pym industry" in both Great Britain and America and mentions papers delivered by Betty Jo McCommas (on the theology of Pym's High Anglicanism), Victoria Glendinning (on "The Pym Man"), Hilary Spurling (on "The Pym Woman"), and Edwin Ardener (on his days as a colleague of Pym's at the International African Institute [*see* 1986.4]).

16 CLAYTON, SYLVIA. "Pym's No. 1." *Punch* 291 (13 August):44.

Review of *An Academic Question.* Agrees that this is a "transitional work, less cosy than her previous books," but that it adds to the Pym collection of "pompous men and pushy women." Praises her powers of observation and mentions *Excellent Women, An Unsuitable Attachment,* and *Jane and Prudence.*

17 COOLEY, MASON. "*The Sweet Dove Died:* The Sexual Politics of Narcissism." *Twentieth Century Literature* 32 (Spring):40-49.

Like *Quartet in Autumn, The Sweet Dove Died* is a masterpiece of "condensation and lucidity." Its plot is built on a series of love triangles and represents "tangled and mismatched loves with great conciseness and richness of implication." But the novel is also Pym's "coldest and most unforgiving." Notes parallels with Jane Austen's *Emma,* Henry James's *Portrait of a Lady* and *Spoils of Poynton,* and D.H. Lawrence's *Women in Love.*

18 DANIEL, MARGARET. "More Excellent Women." *Church Times* (London), 22 August, p. 10.

Review of *An Academic Question.* "No matter what the prevailing morality, Miss Pym's uniquely-observed characters ... are her specialty. And it is the hedgehog enthusiast, the uncertain Caro and the odd-bod academics that make up for any inadequacies in this story and bestow on the book a familiar pleasure."

19 DIGILIO, ALICE. "Barbara Pym's Faculty Party." *Washington Post Book World,* 28 September, p. 9.

Review of *An Academic Question.* Comments on Pym's "good-humored yet clear-eyed generosity towards humanity in all its forms." Her characters' capacity for sympathy "gives them a kind of self-containment and confidence that saves them from wimpishness."

20 D[ONAVIN], D[ENISE] P. "Adult Fiction." *Booklist* 82 (August):1663.

Review of *An Academic Question.* Finds the main attraction in the insight this novel provides into "the author's struggles as a novelist." Some of the characters are "charming"; others are "flamboyant and mundane." The controversy over a manuscript enlivens her "typically quiet plot."

21 DORRIS, MICHAEL. *"An Academic Question* by Barbara Pym." *Los Angeles Times Book Review,* 14 September, p. 6.

Review of *An Academic Question.* "Thanks to the seemingly effortless grace of Pym's language and to the deadpan gaze with which she approaches her subject, the reader is involved almost as a participant in the milieu of the author's invention." Although the flow of the novel is "occasionally choppy," the novel offers revelations into the possibility of Pym's own frustration as an unappreciated author. "It was her special genius to expose the sweetness, the urgency, the silliness and the significance of small events, and, in so doing, to transform them into art."

22 EPSTEIN, JOSEPH. "Miss Pym and Mr. Larkin." *Quadrant* 30 (December):9-17.

Pym and Larkin and the decay of British culture as described in their works. Both Pym and Philip Larkin create art in which "technique never overwhelms content. It is an art in which the ironic, the comic, the understated, the fearlessly honest are given full play, while the shocking and the deliberately hideous are excluded. Excitement in such an art derives from precision of language and subtlety of sentiment, not from tension."

23 FRANCIS, JOHN. "What about the Clergy?" *Southern Evening Echo* (London), 6 September, p. 4.

Brief review of *An Academic Question.* Laments the absence of clergymen in this novel. "Slim as novels go these days, it contains much nourishment."

24 FULLER, EDMUND. "Tale No. 12: Essentially Pym." *Wall Street Journal,* 9 September, p. 26.
     Brief review of *An Academic Question.* Finds here "the authentic Pym voice and tone" as well as "abundant brief, deft, characterizations."

25 GILMAN, JAYNE. "Novels from Oxfordshire." *Oxford Mail,* 2 August, p. 18.
     Brief review of *An Academic Question.* This novel "falls flat." Pym knew best; she never sent it to her publisher. It was her "conscious attempt to break out of the groove in which, she knew herself, her talent really lay."

26 GLASBEY, JOANNE. "Fiction." *Time Out,* 13 August, p. 45.
     Review of *An Academic Question.* "Young people, I suspect, will not take kindly to this novel. Like her other writing, while avoiding the coy, its cosy proximity to clergymen and slightly wayward folk failing to connect will frustrate. But as a readable vignette of a certain type of middle-class English life that must surely be diminishing, then it is fairly absorbing, and will be read in decades hence for its good writing."

27 GOFF, MARTYN. "Vital Vignettes." *Daily Telegraph* (London), 1 August, p. 16.
     Review of *An Academic Question.* Recommends this as "a readable and enjoyable novel." Pym's observations of "people, their motives and their surroundings, is sharp and perceptive. The dialogue gives the illusion of being everyday, and often banal, and to achieve that is a skill all of its own."

28 HARVEY, ANNE. "In a Minor Key." *Tablet,* 13 September, p. 959-60.
     Review of *An Academic Question.* Calls the novel "a shortish, easy read; at times the teasing situations seemed to demand a harder bite. . . . Gentle and understating, Barbara Pym once again makes her distinctive mark."

29 HORAN, DAVID. "Aces in the Lively Pack." *Oxford Times,* 5 September, p. 12.
     Brief review of *An Academic Question.* Sees this as "a link between the cosy books of her first flush and the darker novels of her last period." Comments on the recognizable world of "self-absorbed academics and university small-talk."

30 HOWELL, GEORGINA. "Worldly Wise." *Sunday Times* (London), 7
June, pp. 15, 18.
Interview with Hazel Holt and her son, Tom. Comments that
Pym helped her to be "quite good at editing and criticism." Tom
remembers Pym as a "very quiet, unassuming friend" of his mother's.

31 INGRAMS, LUCY. "A Thoroughly Modern Couple." *Literary Review*
85 (September):7-8.
Review of *An Academic Question*. Calls the plot "a sort of lighthearted version" of Henry James's *The Aspern Papers*. But Pym's
interest here is more in comedy than in morals, and her eccentric
characters are particularly entertaining. Calls it a flawed novel and
recommends it to those readers already acquainted with her work, who
will enjoy the main body of the novel as "exquisitely wry and amusing,
. . . poking fun at the drabness and egocentricity that pervades modern
academic institutions."

32 KAUFMAN, ANTHONY. "The Short Fiction of Barbara Pym."
Twentieth Century Literature 32 (Spring):50-77.
Demonstrates how Pym's "preoccupation with kinds of failure"
can be seen in her short fiction; often she creates a protagonist "who in
one way or another must settle for something less than what is
satisfactory or even necessary." Notes in the stories certain "repetitive
patterns" that go beyond what is understood to be "very Barbara
Pym." Covers "The Day the Music Came," "Goodbye Balkan Capital,"
"Something to Remember," "English Ladies," "Across a Crowded
Room," "The White Elephant," as well as the radio play, "Parrots'
Eggs: An Anthropological Comedy," and two comic pieces, "The
Rectory (or Any Other Title You Like!)" and "The Christmas Visit."
Includes mention of *Some Tame Gazelle, Excellent Women, Jane and
Prudence, Quartet in Autumn, Crampton Hodnet,* and *An Unsuitable
Attachment.* Concludes that Pym fulfilled her desire to create a
fictional world expressed in her own style. "The unpublished short
fiction, varied though its accomplishments may be, succeeds best when
expressing the subjects that most fascinated [her] and which she re-
created from first to last in her career as a novelist."

33 KEATES, JONATHAN. "Out of Her Depth." *Observer* (London), 3
August, p. 23.
Review of *An Academic Question*. This novel "all too easily
underlines its author's shortcomings," including "a severe narrowness
of vision and intellect" that "invalidates" any comparison with Jane
Austen. The writing is "strangely tired, acrid, half-hearted."

34 KEMP, PETER. "Disappointments and Dashed Hopes." *Sunday Times* (London), 27 July, p. 50.

Review of *An Academic Question*. Notes the novel's "loose ends," "superfluous-seeming characters," "desultory episodes," and "dated" picture of campus life, and yet finds appeal in Pym's "distinctive wit and watchfulness."

35 KEMPF, ANDREA CARON. "Adult Fiction." *Library Journal* 111 (August):172.

Review of *An Academic Question*. This novel will not enhance Pym's reputation. "Absent is [her] genius for creating characters whose concerns, no matter how trivial, engage the reader. Her fans, however, will probably demand the book."

36 KING, FRANCIS. "Not Quietly Desperate but Defiantly Humorous." *Spectator* 257 (2 August):23-24.

Review of *An Academic Question*. Responds to Anita Brookner's general appraisal of Pym (*see* 1986.13), saying that she went astray in assuming that Pym's life was "one of quiet desperation." Sees this novel as Pym's attempt to "move out of the narrow territory of the spinster novel." Sadly, this is not a "novel of distinction."

37 KITCHEN, MARGARET. "Pym Special." *Daily Post* (London), 7 August, p. 3.

Review of *An Academic Question*. Says the husband and wife in this novel come across as "rather stiff and unreal." The eccentrics, on the other hand, "are again the real stuff" of the story. Missing is "the depth of Austen-like humour" we have come to expect from Pym. But this is a "welcome addition" to her work.

38 LASKI, MARGHANITA. "Pastel Palettes." *Country Life,* 11 September, p. 790.

Review of *An Academic Question*. Expresses pleasure with the setting (a refreshing change from "two or three families in a country village"), the irony ("somewhat sharper than usual"), and the minor characters ("well and clearly painted"). Had Pym "written more sturdily and determinedly against the grain" she might have been led to a valuable breakthrough.

39 LONG, ROBERT EMMET. *Barbara Pym.* New York: Ungar, 200 pp.

Studies Pym's life and career. In the first of seven chapters, draws on *A Very Private Eye,* selected material in the Oxford Pym papers, and correspondence with the late Lord David Cecil. Treats the first eleven novels, paying particular attention to the recurrence of certain themes and character types, to her modes of social comedy and satire, to her pervasive concern with "unrealized" love and solitude. Considers the "ironic romances" in *Excellent Women, A Glass of Blessings,* and *Quartet in Autumn* her greatest triumphs. Concludes by noting the way in which Jane Austen's dynamic English provincial world has reached a point of breakdown in Pym. (*See* 1986.13)

40 LOPEZ, RUTH. "Encore for Fans of Pym." *Chicago Tribune Book World,* 26 August, p. 3.
Review of *An Academic Question.* Of all her novels, this one comes the closest to reflecting Pym's personal life.

41 LYLES, JEAN CAFFEY. "Pym's Cup: Anglicans and Anthropologists." *Christian Century* 103 (21 May):519-22.
Discusses all of Pym's novels in light of her interest in the church and anthropology. "Pym's unique way of expressing her love was to entertain us, while reminding us, gently but pointedly, of our foibles."

42 MADDOX, BRENDA. "Niminy-Pyminy." *Sunday Telegraph* (London), 3 August, p. 17.
Review of *An Academic Question.* In spite of the novel's shallow characters, repetitions, and coincidences, the story works. "This posthumous patchwork is a risk well taken and has produced a story which, in its unassuming way, is full of suspense." Disagrees that Pym is a second Jane Austen. "The sense of failure hangs too heavily over [her] small worlds."

43 MAROWSKI, DANIEL G., ed. "Pym, Barbara (1913-1980)." In *Contemporary Literary Criticism: Excerpts from Criticism of the Works of Today's Novelists, Poets, Playwrights, Short Story Writers, Scriptwriters, and Other Creative Writers.* Detroit: Gale, pp. 367-80.
Includes biographical sketch, overview of Pym's career, and excerpts of: 1981.13, 18, 23, 27; 1982.13-14, 16, 19, 42, 47; 1983.31, 37, 64-65, 68; 1984.35, 64, 67, 85; 1985.5, 9, 17, 36.

44 MASSIE, ALLAN. "A Question Better Left Unanswered." *Scotsman* (Edinburgh), 16 August, p. 3.
Review of *An Academic Question.* Given the history of this novel, we should not expect it will be very good, and it isn't. Pym's plan to make this into "a sort of Margaret Drabble effort" was obviously mistaken, because "her own characteristic virtues dimmed." Thus the portrait of Caro is "unconvincing," the academic question of the title is

"silly," and nothing is made of two characters who are introduced in the first pages of the novel. "It was, I think, a mistake to publish this novel [because it draws] attention to her very limited emotional range and the narrow nature of her achievement."

45 O'BRIEN, ROBERT. "What Message Comes Across?" *Standard* (London), 30 July, p. 11.

Brief review of *An Academic Question*. Says the novel offers "neither a deft satirical touch nor a particularly subtle insight."

46 O'CONNOR, PATRICIA T. "New and Noteworthy." *New York Times Book Review,* 7 December, p. 82.

Review of *Crampton Hodnet*. "Pym brings together many of the characters and settings . . . that become familiar in her later works."

47 PULSIFER, GARY. "English Fiction." *British Book News,* October, p. 601.

Review of *An Academic Question*. Considers this an admirable combination of two versions of the same novel. Finds it "very funny," but upon finishing it, finds he wants "a bit more substance."

48 RAPHAEL, ISABEL. "Cool Pym's Number Seven." *Times* (London), 31 July, p. 13.

Review of *An Academic Question*. On first reading, this novel is "thin" and lacks the "cool formality and decorum" that attract readers to the postwar novels. On second reading, one can appreciate Pym's "shrewd" observations, humor, and "gentle cattiness . . . which beautifully deflates academic pretension and puts social trendiness in its place. Not vintage Pym, but a solid addition to the canon."

49 RUBENSTEIN, JILL. " 'For the Ovaltine Had Loosened Her Tongue': Failures of Speech in Barbara Pym's *Less Than Angels*." *Modern Fiction Studies* 32 (Winter):573-80.

Examines the "failures of interpretation and infelicities of speech acts" in *Less Than Angels*. This problem is the primary source of both comedy and gloom in Pym's vision of human relations.

50 RUBIN, MERLE. "A Cooler, Tougher Woman." *New York Times Book Review,* 7 September, p. 25.

Review of *An Academic Question*. Calls this one of Pym's "paler efforts" but interesting "in its own right . . . and for the insight it provides about what can happen when a writer tries to work against her grain."

51 SACKVILLE-WEST, SARAH. "Sipping Gently at the Latest Pym."
Catholic Herald, 15 August, p. 9.

Review of *An Academic Question.* Although Pym sought to
broaden her scope with this novel, finds here the familiar pattern of
characters and themes. "As always, [this novel] is hugely readable and
entertaining, with the Pym touches of domestic humour, the gentle yet
astute observations of human character and the richness of detail,
conspiring to make it a work well up to her usual excellence."

52 SEYMOUR-SMITH, MARTIN. "Born of Rejection." *Financial Times*
(London), 2 September, p. 27.

Review of *An Academic Question.* Calls the book "a series of
exquisitely small observations strung together on a clumsy thread of a
psychologically unconvincing story." Doubts that Pym is the most
underrated writer of the century. "Pym just did not have the
imagination or the art to write the novel she might have written about
her own sense of disappointment: her plots are always obtrusively
clumsy, and she strained after an understanding she did not have
instead of writing about its bitter consequences."

53 SHAPIRO, LAURA. "Footnotes." *Newsweek* 108 (10 November):84.

Review of *An Academic Question.* Calls the novel "slightly more
acid" than Pym's other work but provides her "characteristic wit."
Finds that the author's "tilt toward benevolence, along with a penchant
for skewering her characters as if they were so many chunks of
marinated beef, makes Pym a classic storyteller – and a powerful
addiction."

54 SHRAPNEL, NORMAN. "Making Victims." *Guardian* (Manchester),
1 August, p. 19.

Review of *An Academic Question.* Senses that Pym was uncertain
about her tone, but in a way this helps her heroine, Caroline, "who also
lacks assurance and regards her academic husband with rather the
same nervous suspicion that Miss Pym had learned to apply to her own
fickle public."

55 STUTTAFORD, GENEVIEVE. "PW Forecasts: Fiction." *Publishers
Weekly* 230 (11 July):53-54.

Review of *An Academic Question.* "The depth and variety of this
posthumous novel confirms that Pym's so-called comedies of manners
are serious, challenging works that have much to say about how – with
unquenchable spirit – individuals respond to the indignities of
emotional isolation, rejection and loss." Sees this as a "natural bridge"

between the early and late work. Praises the "finely etched" characters and the "small but meaningful" plot twists.

56 TAYLOR, D.J. "Recent Fiction." *Encounter* 67 (June):53-54.
    Review of *Crampton Hodnet*. "Behind the genteel frontage there is a sharper, harsher writer trying to get out." Calls this "slyly plotted" novel "an odd mixture of jauntiness and cynicism." Overenthusiastic admirers may jeopardize her reputation.

57 WAUGH, HARRIET. "Recent Fiction: Promoting the Pym Industry." *Illustrated London News* 274 (October):80.
    Review of *An Academic Question*. Does not think Pym's reputation will be well served by the promotion of a literary industry around her. To publish a novel that had been rejected by the author herself is "morally reprehensible." But the novel is enjoyable reading, "still superior to a good many novels that come my way."

58 WILCE, GILLIAN. "Ghost Story." *New Statesman* 112 (15 August):31.
    Review of *An Academic Question*. Finds that the tone and characterization are "distinctly Pymish" but there is an air of unreality about the novel, "as if the characters had been transposed into the wrong environment." Calls this "a shadow of Pym's best work" and questions the wisdom of publishing "a minor, unfinished, not wholly satisfying novel of hers now."

59 WOODFORDE, JOHN. "Miss Pym Passes By." *Sunday Telegraph* (London), 8 July, p. 27.
    Reports on a radio documentary, "The World of Barbara Pym," in which her sister and various friends reminisced and read from extracts and diaries.

1987

1 ANON. "Fiction." *Kirkus Reviews* 55 (1 November):1537.
    Review of *Civil to Strangers and Other Writings*. Questions the value of this collection. The four stories do not show Pym at her best. The two romances are "joyless" and the spy story is rather clumsy. The interview seems "airless and unenlightening."

2 ANON. "PW Forecasts: Fiction." *Publishers Weekly* 232 (20 November):61.
    Review of *Civil to Strangers and Other Writings*. Finds foreshadowed here Pym's "fine career." Praises "Across a Crowded

Room" as the "most luminous" of the writing. A "fuller picture" of Pym at work emerges from these pieces.

3 BACHELDER, FRANCES H. "The Importance of Connecting." In *The Life and Work of Barbara Pym*. Edited by Dale Salwak. London: Macmillan; Iowa City: University of Iowa Press, pp. 185-92.

Seeks to show that each of Pym's eleven novels is a vital part of the whole picture and therefore dependent on the others for a better understanding of the life-style she portrays: "all similar, but, like stitches in a hand-knitted sweater, each is slightly different and therein lies the beauty of the human touch."

4 BAILEY, HILARY. "Other Worlds and Ours." *Guardian* (London), 27 November, p. 24.

Brief review of *Civil to Strangers and Other Writings*. Says it is a pity there isn't more of "So Very Secret." Thinks it would be interesting to see how Pym "might have dealt with a scene where, say, a German spy disguised as a curate emerged from the dripping rhododendrons with a Luger in his hand."

5 BAYLEY, JOHN. "Where, Exactly, Is the Pym World?" In *The Life and Work of Barbara Pym*. Edited by Dale Salwak. London: Macmillan; Iowa City: University of Iowa Press, pp. 50-57.

Explains how Pym's work eludes any definition in terms of novelistic convention, description, and methodology. There is really no such thing as a "Barbara Pym world." That is the final paradox about her and the final triumph of her art.

6 BRADHAM, MARGARET C. "Barbara Pym's Women." *World Literature Today* 61 (Winter):31-37.

Discusses Pym's treatment of women in the first ten novels.

7 BURKHART, CHARLES. *The Pleasure of Miss Pym*. Austin: University of Texas Press, 120 pp.

Discusses her life and autobiographical writings as well as her fiction through *An Academic Question*. Focuses on her worldview, the unique nature of her comedy, her religion, her place within the history of the novel, and her insights into male-female relationships. Includes photographs.

8 De PAULO, ROSEMARY. "You Are What You Drink." *Barbara Pym Newsletter* 2 (December):1-5.

Treats drinking and its relation to characterization and social class in Pym's novels.

9 GLEN, CAVALIERO. "Pym Again." *Country Life,* 24 December, p. 8.

Review of *Civil to Strangers and Other Writings.* Finds "Gervase and Flora" "mordant and disquieting" and of some biographical importance. The unfinished novel *Home Front Novel* is characteristically underplayed, but *So Very Secret* shows more originality, offers "great fun," and calls to mind the early films of Alfred Hitchcock.

10 GODWIN, GAIL. "Years of Neglect." In *The Life and Work of Barbara Pym.* Edited by Dale Salwak. London: Macmillan; Iowa City: University of Iowa Press, p. 193.

Brief tribute to Pym whose "valiantly civilised and unpretentious landscapes remain vividly before us." Calls *A Very Private Eye* "engrossing and poignant."

11 GORRA, MICHAEL. "The Sun Never Sets on the English Novel." *New York Times Book Review,* 19 July, p. 24.

In discussing the vitality of today's English novel, notes the entertainment it affords in novelists like Pym and Margaret Drabble, who face up to the novel's conventionality and accept its "modest place in what Miss Drabble has called a 'dying tradition.' "

12 GRAHAM, ROBERT J. "The Narrative Sense of Barbara Pym." In *The Life and Work of Barbara Pym.* Edited by Dale Salwak. London: Macmillan; Iowa City: University of Iowa Press, pp. 142-55.

Presents a full picture of the general function and subtleties of Pym's narrator in *Excellent Women, Less Than Angels, No Fond Return of Love, Quartet in Autumn,* and *The Sweet Dove Died.*

13 GRONER, MARLENE SAN MIGUEL. "Barbara Pym's Allusions to Seventeenth-Century Poets." *Cross Bias: Newsletter of Friends of Bemerton,* November, pp. 5-7.

Identifies and discusses the significance of allusions to metaphysical poetry in Pym's novels.

14 HALPERIN, JOHN. "Barbara Pym and the War of the Sexes." In *The Life and Work of Barbara Pym.* Edited by Dale Salwak. London: Macmillan; Iowa City: University of Iowa Press, pp. 88-100.

Seeks to answer the question of why men find Pym's books very sad and women don't by examining the relationships between the sexes in *Excellent Women, Jane and Prudence, Less Than Angels, The Sweet Dove Died,* and *An Unsuitable Attachment.* Pym sees an imbalance in control or power, whether romantic or familial, between the sexes. Men think women are too strong; women think men are too strong.

15 HAMILTON-SMITH, BARBARA. "Another Day, Another Pym's Oates." *Catholic Herald,* 30 January, p. 12.
    Review of *An Academic Question.* Calls this "a refreshing novel in the best Pym tradition of wry humour and mild eccentricity."

16 HAZZARD, SHIRLEY. "Excellent Woman." In *The Life and Work of Barbara Pym.* Edited by Dale Salwak. London: Macmillan; Iowa City: University of Iowa Press, p. 3.
    Brief tribute to Pym's "strong original view." Mentions *Excellent Women.*

17 HEBERLEIN, KATE BROWDER. "Thankless Tasks or Labors of Love: Women's Work in Barbara Pym's Novels." *Barbara Pym Newsletter* 2 (June):1-5.
    Discusses Pym's treatment of women's work in the novels.

18 HILLS, C.A.R. "The Bubble, Reputation: The Decline and Rise of Barbara Pym." *Encounter* 68 (May):33-38.
    Offers an overview of all twelve novels and *A Very Private Eye.* Discusses Pym's comedy and often deep melancholy. Considers the reasons she was neglected by publishers.

19 HOLT, HAZEL. "No Thankless Task: Barbara Pym as Indexer." *Indexer* 15 (October):236-37.
    Memoir of Pym's enjoyment of the art of indexing with the International African Institute's publications. Apart from putting words in a certain order, what she most enjoyed was "the peaceful, enclosed *space* an indexer inhabits."

20 _____. "The Novelist in the Field: 1946-1974." In *The Life and Work of Barbara Pym.* Edited by Dale Salwak. London: Macmillan; Iowa City: University of Iowa Press, pp. 22-33.
    Relives her years at the International African Institute in London, where Holt was editorial secretary and assistant editor of the journal *Africa* and close friend and literary adviser to Pym.

21 H[OOPER], B[RAD]. "Literature." *Booklist* 84 (1 December):602.
Review of *Civil to Strangers and Other Writings*. "The reason Pym has such a large audience – her subtle but warm and moving ability to create idiosyncratic but perfectly embraceable and entertaining characters – is fully observable here." *Civil to Strangers* is a "delightful" novel. The short stories are not perfect but "certainly interesting."

22 HUTH, ANGELA. "Cups of Tea and Dishy Men." *Sunday Telegraph* (London), 27 December, p. 11.
Review of *Civil to Strangers and Other Writings*. Praises the author's "premature maturity" in *Civil to Strangers* and says that its "quiet suspense, till all ends morally right, is captivating." *Gervase and Flora* is "thinly disguised truth" about unrequited love. *Home Front Novel* is "evocative." The Enid Blyton plot in *So Very Secret* is "hilarious." Of the short stories, "Across a Crowded Room" is the "most successful."

23 LARKIN, PHILIP. "The Rejection of Barbara Pym." In *The Life and Work of Barbara Pym*. Edited by Dale Salwak. London: Macmillan; Iowa City: University of Iowa Press, pp. 171-75.
Reprint of 1982.39.

24 LIDDELL, ROBERT. "A Success Story." In *The Life and Work of Barbara Pym*. Edited by Dale Salwak. London: Macmillan; Iowa City: University of Iowa Press, pp. 176-84.
Considers critical misconceptions that Pym was "frustrated" or that she "wasted her affections on unworthy people." Turns to the novels to "correct any false impressions" derived from *A Very Private Eye*.

25 LIVELY, PENELOPE. "The World of Barbara Pym." In *The Life and Work of Barbara Pym*. Edited by Dale Salwak. London: Macmillan; Iowa City: University of Iowa Press, pp. 45-49.
Reprint of 1980.53.

26 MacKAY, SHENA. "Books of the Year." *Sunday Times* (London), 29 November, p. 5.
Cites *Civil to Strangers and Other Writings* for its "reassuring English melancholy, vivid imagery and lethal humour, and its account of its author's exile in the literary wilderness."

27 ____. "Hissing Tea-urns and Sensuous Hearts." *Sunday Times* (London), 29 November, p. 5.

Review of *Civil to Strangers and Other Writings*. Expresses sadness that this is the last collection of Pym's uncollected work. Miss Morrow and Miss Doggett (in "So, Some Tempestuous Morn") are "archetypal Pym inventions." *So Very Secret* is not only "almost documentary in its detail" but also "extremely funny" and profound in its truthfulness.

28 MALLOY, CONSTANCE. "The Quest for a Career." In *The Life and Work of Barbara Pym*. Edited by Dale Salwak. London: Macmillan; Iowa City: University of Iowa Press, pp. 4-21.
    Overview of Pym's life and career.

29 OATES, JOYCE CAROL. "Barbara Pym's Novelistic Genius." In *The Life and Work of Barbara Pym*. Edited by Dale Salwak. London: Macmillan; Iowa City: University of Iowa Press, pp. 43-44.
    Brief tribute to Pym's "inimitable quality of personality that shines through the carefully wrought, understated prose, blossoming now and then in marvellous surprising perceptions." Cites *Excellent Women* and *Jane and Prudence* as her favorite novels.

30 PHELPS, GILBERT. "Fellow Writers in a Cotswold Village." In *The Life and Work of Barbara Pym*. Edited by Dale Salwak. London: Macmillan; Iowa City: University of Iowa Press, pp. 34-39.
    Discusses his friendship with Pym, including some critical comments on her work and the climate of English criticism that led to her long neglect.

31 PICKERING, SAM. "Writers Reading." *Horizon* 30 (October):63.
    Says that Pym writes like Austen: "elegant, graceful novels about contemporary village life in rural England." Praises *Excellent Women* and *Quartet in Autumn*.

32 POLSTER, ERVING. *Every Person's Life Is Worth a Novel*. New York and London: Norton, pp. 149-50.
    Comments on the "transformation of the mundane into the fascinating" in *Excellent Women*. Mildred Lathbury's new neighbors "implant new liveliness in her consciousness." At first a dull woman, she becomes "a woman of individuality and excitement ... through new opportunities and stimulation." Finds in this experience an analogy to therapy, in which the therapist "offers a new presence in his patients' lives."

33 PROKOP, MARY K. "Fiction." *Library Journal* 112 (15 November):91.

Review of *Civil to Strangers and Other Writings*. Comments on the short stories ("delightful"), *So Very Secret* ("surprisingly entertaining"), and "Finding a Voice: A Radio Talk" ("quite appealing"). Although this collection is not Pym at her "zenith," it is "awfully good."

34 RAPHAEL, ISABEL. "Wild Shore of Love." *Times* (London), 5 November, p. 17.

Review of *Civil to Strangers and Other Writings*. Only Pym's most dedicated fans will find much to reward them in this collection. *Home Front Novel* has "tantalizing possibilities." *So Very Secret* is "quite terrible."

35 ROSSEN, JANICE. "The Pym Papers." In *The Life and Work of Barbara Pym*. Edited by Dale Salwak. London: Macmillan; Iowa City: University of Iowa Press, pp. 156-67.

Offers a detailed description of the Pym papers held at the Bodleian Library, Oxford.

36 _____. *The World of Barbara Pym*. London: Macmillan; New York: St. Martin's Press, 193 pp.

Focuses on twentieth-century England as Pym saw, lived, satirized, and enjoyed it. Draws from a reading of the author's private papers and conversations with many who knew her. Defines Pym's significance within the framework of the modern British novel, traces her artistic development, explores relationship between her life and fiction, and addresses broader themes regarding British culture in her work, such as spinsterhood, anthropology, English literature, the Anglican church, and Oxford University.

37 ROWSE, A.L. "Miss Pym and Miss Austen." In *The Life and Work of Barbara Pym*. Edited by Dale Salwak. London: Macmillan; Iowa City: University of Iowa Press, pp. 64-71.

Considers similarities between Pym and Austen: "their relation to the society of their times, and their rendering of each." Concludes that both authors "are well worthy of each other; they were both moral perfectionists, both perfect artists."

38 SAAR, DOREEN ALVAREZ. "Irony from a Female Perspective: A Study of the Early Novels of Barbara Pym." *West Virginia University Philological Papers* 33 (June):68-75.

Considers the development of themes, characters, and social views in the first six novels.

39 SALWAK, DALE, ed. *The Life and Work of Barbara Pym*. London: Macmillan; Iowa City: University of Iowa Press, 210 pp.

Nineteen essays examine Pym's life and work. Part I, "The Life": Shirley Hazzard, Hazel Holt, Constance Malloy, Gilbert Phelps. Part II, "The Work": John Bayley, Robert J. Graham, John Halperin, Penelope Lively, Joyce Carol Oates, Janice Rossen, A.L. Rowse, Muriel Schulz, Robert Smith, Lotus Snow, Mary Strauss-Noll. Part III, "In Retrospect": Frances H. Bachelder, Gail Godwin, Philip Larkin, Robert Liddell. Includes primary bibliography, select secondary bibliography, and index.

40 SCHULZ, MURIEL. "The Novelist as Anthropologist." In *The Life and Work of Barbara Pym*. Edited by Dale Salwak. London: Macmillan; Iowa City: University of Iowa Press, pp. 101-119.

Anthropologists appear in many of Pym's novels, as does her sense of amusement at anthropologists believing they must travel so far from home to find interesting cultures to study. In so doing they leave for the novelist the study of the everyday life of English men and women, a study Pym pursued in the novels written during her years at the International African Institute.

41 SHERWOOD, RHODA IRENE. " 'A Special Kind of Double': Sisters in British and American Fiction." Ph.D. dissertation, University of Wisconsin, 164 pp.

Some Tame Gazelle depicts some of the more pleasant features of sisterhood. "Pym spoofs romantic comedy and suggests that blessed as the wedded woman may be, more blessed still is the spinster who shares with her sister fantasies about romance and quiet and pleasantly predictable routine."

42 SHULMAN, NICOLA. "To Marry or to Smoulder Gently." *Times Literary Supplement*, 25 December, p. 1420.

Review of *Civil to Strangers and Other Writings*. Considers *Some Tame Gazelle*, *An Unsuitable Attachment*, *Jane and Prudence*, *Less Than Angels*, and the collected writings to demonstrate that the war between the sexes is at the core of Pym's work. "Pym's novels and stories reveal the battle but obscure the victor: it is not, ultimately, clear which sex has the upper hand. Her comic, forgiving vision of men and women's failure to come to terms with one another hits as near the truth as that of much greater novelists." The same "inconclusive subtlety" is found in Edith Wharton.

43 SIMMONS, JAMES. "Excess and Reticence." *Spectator* 260 (2 January):24.

Review of *Civil to Strangers and Other Writings. Civil to Strangers* ("a dream of modest felicity") seems "trivial and uncertain" at the start because Pym mocks the limitations of her characters, but eventually she seems to respect her characters and "so does the reader." Finds that Pym has "just enough vision to sustain her observations and narrative skills." *Gervase and Flora* is a "swift and delicate" story. Notes parallels between Pym's heroines and Olivia Manning's.

44 SMITH, ROBERT. "How Pleasant to Know Miss Pym." In *The Life and Work of Barbara Pym.* Edited by Dale Salwak. London: Macmillan; Iowa City: University of Iowa Press, pp. 58-63.

Reprint of 1971.1.

45 SNOW, LOTUS. "Literary Allusions in the Novels." In *The Life and Work of Barbara Pym.* Edited by Dale Salwak. London: Macmillan; Iowa City: University of Iowa Press, pp. 120-41.

Discusses the abundance of literary allusions and quotations that filter through the minds of Pym's characters. Examines what the allusions reveal about the characters' interior worlds as well as the novels' themes. Reprinted: 1987.46.

46 ____. *One Little Room an Everywhere: Barbara Pym's Novels.* Orono, Maine: Puckerbrush Press, 101 pp.

In seven chapters discusses Pym's interest in ordinary people and their mundane lives, her selection of names for her characters (incorporating many literary allusions), her presentation of men (who "take for granted their superiority to women; they enjoy a sense of martyrdom in their professions; they lack both sensitivity and subtlety; and they exploit the myth of their helplessness"), and married women. Includes reprint of 1980.71; 1987.45.

47 STRAUSS-NOLL, MARY [THERESE]. "Love and Marriage in the Novels." In *The Life and Work of Barbara Pym.* Edited by Dale Salwak. London: Macmillan; Iowa City: University of Iowa Press, pp. 72-87.

Examines both the published and unpublished works to show that "the ambivalence of the single women and the disillusionment of the married women occur throughout all Pym's writings." Concludes that "together or separately, love and marriage are usually considered mixed blessings" in the novels.

48 TOMALIN, CLAIRE. "Wife Support System." *Observer* (London), 15 November, p. 26.

Review of *Civil to Strangers and Other Writings*. Beneath Pym's "wit and melancholy, there is something profoundly reassuring about her picture of the world." That reassurance lies in the "essential role of *all* the women" in her writings. Comments on "Across a Crowded Room" (poignant because based on a true incident involving Larkin), *Civil to Strangers,* "Goodbye Balkan Capital" ("superb war story"), and "Finding a Voice: A Radio Talk." Says that Pym wrote about "people who expect to be slighted and are; but her tone is never indignant."

49 WYMARD, ELEANOR B. "Barbara Pym on Organized Religion: A Case of Folly." *Month* 258 (August/September):318-20.

Examines the serious religious concerns in the first eleven novels. Because her characters are disappointed with organized religion in times of need, they "devise their own ceremonies in order to experience renewal." She treats religion as a "secular phenomenon" and challenges "its decline as a mere product of human culture." Compares her view with those of Graham Greene, Evelyn Waugh, Muriel Spark, and Anthony Trollope. Pym sees day-to-day life in "religious, but non-institutional terms." The "essential folly" of the church contributes to the tension and comedy of Pym's world.

1988

1 ACKLEY, KATHERINE ANNE. "But What Does It Lead To?" *Barbara Pym Newsletter* 3 (December):3-5.

The most forceful argument in favor of literature is seen in Pym's treatment of the contrast between anthropologists and writers. Discusses *A Few Green Leaves, An Unsuitable Attachment,* and *Less Than Angels*. Throughout her novels she implies that "it gives consolation and pain, it helps people connect to one another, it liberates the spirit, and it ultimately makes its readers more compassionate human beings."

2 ANON. "Bookends." *Time* 131 (29 February):100.

Review of *Civil to Strangers and Other Writings*. Finds everywhere in this collection "the unmistakable Pym piquancy." Calls Pym the last of the line of "dryly insightful spinsters," which may be traced back to Jane Austen. This collection and her previous books "show how much the type is to be missed."

3 ANON. "Briefly Noted: Fiction." *New Yorker* 64 (22 February):117.
Brief review of *Civil to Strangers and Other Writings*. Some of this "welcome" collection's finest passages are found in "Goodbye Balkan Capital" and *Home Front Novel*. Hazel Holt's introductory comments are "impeccable, and her editing seems judicious and discreet."

4 ANON. "Paperbacks." *Observer* (London), 14 February, p. 27.
Review of *An Academic Question*. "Campus shenanigans were not her thing, but fans will twitter admiringly." Calls the novel an "unsuccessful attempt at artistic bra-burning."

5 BAYLEY, JOHN. "From the Battlefield of Society." *Times Literary Supplement*, 1 April, p. 347.
Refers to Huxley's *Crome Yellow* as the catalyst that started Pym writing novels.

6 BOWMAN, BARBARA. "Barbara Pym's Subversive Subtext: Private Irony and Shared Detachment." In *Independent Women: The Function of Gender in the Novels of Barbara Pym*. Edited by Janice Rossen. Sussex: Harvester; New York: St. Martin's Press, pp. 82-94.
Examines the divided narrative voice that Pym used to achieve complex characterization in her major female characters and the contrasting single voice assigned to all of the males.

7 BURKHART, CHARLES. "Glamorous Acolytes: Homosexuality in Pym's World." In *Independent Women: The Function of Gender in the Novels of Barbara Pym*. Edited by Janice Rossen. Sussex: Harvester; New York: St. Martin's Press, pp. 95-105.
Focuses on Pym's depictions of bachelors and homosexuals, their dependency on women in the novel, and their sense of humor.

8 DIPPLE, ELIZABETH. *The Unresolvable Plot: Reading Contemporary Fiction*. London and New York: Routledge, pp. 255-56.
Discusses briefly the similarities between Pym and Doris Lessing. *The Diaries of Jane Somers* are "informed with ethical intention beyond Pym's gentle depictions of lonely women."

9 DOAN, LAURA L. "Text and the Single Man: The Bachelor in Pym's Dual-Voiced Narrative." In *Independent Women: The Function of Gender in the Novels of Barbara Pym*. Edited by Janice Rossen. Sussex: Harvester; New York: St. Martin's Press, pp. 63-81.
Discusses Pym's characterizations of bachelors and homosexuals and their dependency on women.

10 DOBIE, ANN B. "The World of Barbara Pym: Novelist as Anthropologist." *Arizona Quarterly* 44 (Spring):5-18.

Discusses the influence of anthropology on Pym's writings. "Human beings are, in the world of Barbara Pym, poignant in their solitary state, amusing in their pettiness, and admirable in their attempts to transcend their limitations. In her novels they are resilient creatures who quietly battle to realize life's dreams and overcome life's disappointments."

11 EVERETT, BARBARA. "The Pleasures of Poverty." In *Independent Women: The Function of Gender in the Novels of Barbara Pym*. Edited by Janice Rossen. Sussex: Harvester; New York: St. Martin's Press, pp. 9-20.

Reviews Pym's journals, diaries, and *A Very Private Eye* in terms of the events they record that she later adapted for use in her novels. Reprint of 1984.41.

12 FERGUS, JAN. "*A Glass of Blessings,* Jane Austen's *Emma,* and Barbara Pym's Art of Allusion." In *Independent Women: The Function of Gender in the Novels of Barbara Pym*. Sussex: Harvester; New York: St. Martin's Press, pp. 109-36.

Demonstrates that Pym used Jane Austen's *Emma* as a source for the theme and imagery in *A Glass of Blessings*.

13 FISICHELLI, GLYNN-ELLEN [MARIA]. "The Novelist as Anthropologist: Barbara Pym's Fiction: Fieldwork Done at Home." *Papers on Language and Literature* 24 (Fall):431-45.

Examines Pym's "sociological observations" in all her novels. Finds an "artful blending of her imaginative insight with the anthropologist's methods of detached social analysis." This synthesis culminates in *A Few Green Leaves*.

14 HOLT, HAZEL. "The Home Front: Barbara Pym in Oswestry, 1939-1941." In *Independent Women: The Function of Gender in the Novels of Barbara Pym*. Edited by Janice Rossen. Sussex: Harvester; New York: St. Martin's Press, pp. 50-59.

Considers the years that Pym was still living at home with her parents (1939-1941) a seminal period in her development.

15 JACOBS, BRUCE RICHARD. "Elements of Satire in the Novels of Barbara Pym." Ph.D. dissertation, Fordham University, 320 pp.

Examines all of Pym's novels as satiric comedies in which men are "unimaginative, inept and insensitive" toward women; clerics, spouses, and academics are "sadly ineffectual"; and the social institutions of anthropology, Anglicanism, and marriage cannot inspire a society that is "growing increasingly insular and apathetic." Notes in the last four works "darker characterizations and settings and a more pessimistic, overtly critical outlook on modern society." The novels not only entertain us but also change our social attitudes.

16 KAUFMAN, ANTHONY. "Petrified Mimosa." *Barbara Pym Newsletter* 3 (December):1-3.
    Parody of Pym's narratives with all that would be expected in the way of character, conflict, and literary allusion.

17 KENYON, OLGA. *Women Novelists Today: A Survey of English Writing in the Seventies and Eighties.* Sussex: Harvester; New York: St. Martin's Press, pp. 149-50.
    Considers briefly Pym's diversity as a novelist and her contribution to "the representation of female experience and ideology."

18 LA BELLE, JENIJOY. *Herself Beheld: The Literature of the Looking Glass.* Ithaca and London: Cornell University Press, pp. 4-5.
    Considers what happens when a woman looks into a mirror in *The Sweet Dove Died* (flattering image of Leonora) and *Crampton Hodnet* (aged woman's dialogue with the mirror).

19 LAURIE, HILARY. "An Indexer Observes." *Times Literary Supplement* 12 October, p. 231.
    Review of stage adaptation of *No Fond Return of Love* at the All Saints' Arts Centre. The playwright manages to re-create "Pym's witty, waspish, tragi-comic world." Onstage, however, plot is pushed to the front, and Pym's succinct commentary on events is lost "when action and observation merge."

20 MACHESKI, CECILIA. ". . . Elizabeth Taylor (the Novelist, of Course). . . ." *Barbara Pym Newsletter* 3 (June):5-6.
    Seeks to show not only that Taylor and Pym are indebted to Jane Austen but also that both modern writers "see themselves not as descendents or competitors to earlier fictions but as somehow co-existing with them, as if in a timeless sphere."

21 O'CONNOR, PATRICIA T. "Romance Comes to Up Callow." *New York Times Book Review,* 17 January, p. 29.

Review of *Civil to Strangers and Other Writings*. *Civil to Strangers* can take its place alongside Pym's other works "with no apology." Despite their shortcomings, the stories offer what readers love most in Pym: "her humor, her love of detail, the pleasure she took in what she called the 'trivial round and common task.'" What readers cherish most in Pym is here, "in writing that is at once restrained and fluent." Most evident is her "sincere affection for her characters." The final piece, "Finding a Voice: A Radio Talk," shows how she struggled to find a voice of her own.

22 OUSBY, IAN, ed. "Pym, Barbara (Mary Crampton)." In *The Cambridge Guide to Literature in English*. Cambridge: Cambridge University Press, p. 811.
    "All of Pym's books are wistful, delicate comedies with an unsparingly sad undertow."

23 ROSSEN, JANICE, ed. *Independent Women: The Function of Gender in the Novels of Barbara Pym*. Sussex: Harvester; New York: St. Martin's Press, 172 pp.
    Seeks to test Pym's reputation by considering her craftsmanship, the literary influences on her work, and her special use of language. Includes biographical, historical, and feminist approaches that explore her unique creative process as it relates to events in her life. Features essays by Barbara Bowman, Charles Burkhart, Laura L. Doan, Barbara Everett, Jan Fergus, Hazel Holt, Janice Rossen, Robert Smith, Roger Till, and Anne M. Wyatt-Brown.

24 ____. "On Not Being Jane Eyre: The Romantic Heroine in Barbara Pym's Novels." In *Independent Women: The Function of Gender in the Novels of Barbara Pym*. Sussex: Harvester; New York: St. Martin's Press, pp. 137-56.
    "The disquieting lack of comfort she finds in Brontë's novel becomes transformed in Pym's own fiction into a study of alternative renderings of the Jane Eyre story, as she rewrites *Jane Eyre* in at least three different variations." Considers "Something to Remember," *Excellent Women*, and *The Sweet Dove Died*. "Jane Eyre represents for Pym the archetypal romantic heroine, and for this reason she becomes a reference point for Pym's characters."

25 RUBIN, MERLE. "The Luck of the English." *Los Angeles Times Book Review*, 7 February, p. 6.
    Review of *Civil to Strangers and Other Writings*. Finds Pym's distinctive voice in these early pieces. *Civil to Strangers* is "an elegant

blend of freshness and surprising sophistication." Her "Finnish" novel is more poignant.

26 SADLER, LYNN VEACH. "Drabbling in Pym's Garden of the Critics: Asserting One's World." *Barbara Pym Newsletter* 3 (June):1-4.

Notes similarities between Pym and Margaret Drabble, both of whom struggled to assert the primacy of their fictional worlds and their differences from what is delineated by the critics. The effect is "a bonding between author and reader, a good-faith pledge, on the one hand, of the authenticity of the fictional world so created and, on the other, of the acceptance of authenticity." Like Pym, Drabble "has not emerged unscathed in the struggle for legitimacy, for the right kind of audience appeal."

27 SLUNG, MICHAEL. "Barbara Pym: The Quiet Pleasure of Her Company." *Washington Post Book World,* 17 January, pp. 3, 13.

Brief review of *Civil to Strangers and Other Writings.* Finds clear from the start that Pym's voice was her own. Except for some pleasure in *Civil to Strangers,* this collection "contains nothing that anyone but the most diehard Pym pals need to have between hard covers."

28 SMITH, ROBERT. "Remembering Barbara Pym." In *Independent Women: The Function of Gender in the Novels of Barbara Pym.* Edited by Janice Rossen. Sussex: Harvester; New York: St. Martin's Press, pp. 159-63.

Offers a personal reminiscence of his friend from her early days of success.

29 TILL, ROGER. "Coincidence in a Bookshop." In *Independent Women: The Function of Gender in the Novels of Barbara Pym.* Edited by Janice Rossen. Sussex: Harvester; New York: St. Martin's Press, pp. 164-68.

Personal reminiscence.

30 WALL, STEPHEN. "Being Splendid." *London Review of Books* 10 (3 March):10-11.

Review of *Civil to Strangers and Other Writings.* Considers Pym's failure with the short story form. Most of the fragments "look fumbling and will be of interest to enthusiasts only." *Civil to Strangers* shows a "sureness, and lightness, of touch."

31 WATSON, ALETA. "Collection Offers Last, Lovely Taste of Pym Wryness." *San Jose* (Calif.) *Mercury News,* 3 January, p. 18.

Review of *Civil to Strangers and Other Writings*. Although not her best writing, the "fascinating characters and wry observations" will please her readers. The stories offer tantalizing glimpses of the characters who appear in her later novels. "Across a Crowded Room" is the "most compelling" piece, giving the reader a "sympathetic but unsentimental slice of life."

32 WILSON, A.N. *Penfriends from Porlock*. London: Hamish Hamilton, pp. 112-20.
     Includes reprint of 1982.68.

33 WYATT-BROWN, ANNE M. "Ellipsis, Eccentricity and Evasion in the Diaries of Barbara Pym." In *Independent Women: The Function of Gender in the Novels of Barbara Pym*. Edited by Janice Rossen. Sussex: Harvester; New York: St. Martin's Press, pp. 21-49.
     Discovers that in her private, unpublished writings, Pym transformed her experiences as she recorded them.

34 ____. "Late Style in the Novels of Barbara Pym and Penelope Mortimer." *Gerontologist* 28 (June):835-39.
     Considers Pym's treatment of the elderly and aging compared to Penelope Mortimer's.

1989

1 ACKLEY, KATHERINE ANNE. *The Novels of Barbara Pym*. New York: Garland, 206 pp.
     Offers a comprehensive survey. "What one notices about all Pym's novels is the way she rarely presents anyone or any issue as purely good or purely bad, purely right or purely wrong." Considers the primary themes, character types, relationships between men and women, neglected females, isolation and loneliness, optimism and affirmation of life, and use of literature as a backdrop for the characters' lives. Includes index.

2 ANON. "Fiction." *Washington Post Book World*, 12 February, p. 12.
     Brief review of *Civil to Strangers and Other Writings*. Likes the interview, in which Pym discusses "the joys and terrors of the writer's life."

3 BEISWENGER, ELEANOR. "Teaching Barbara Pym in Britain." *Barbara Pym Newsletter* 4 (December):8-10.

Reports on her experience as a faculty member in the Cooperative Center for Study in Britain during the summer of 1989. Includes "Course Requirements," "Teaching the Novel of Manners," "Some Surprises," "The Advantages of Being in Britain," "Looking for Barbara Pym," "Oswestry," "A Warm Welcome at Morda Lodge," and "Oswestry Itself."

4 BROOKE-ROSE, CHRISTINE. "Illiterations." In *Breaking the Silence: Women's Experimental Fiction.* Introduced and edited by Ellen G. Friedman and Miriam Fuchs. Princeton: Princeton University Press, p. 56.

Brief reference to Pym's difficulties in getting published. Like Jean Rhys, Christina Stead, Ivy Compton-Burnett, Isak Dinesen, and Nathalie Sarraute, she received "the accolade of serious recognition very late in life."

5 COTSELL, MICHAEL. *Barbara Pym.* London: Macmillan; New York: St. Martin's Press, 153 pp.

Examines all of the novels, paying particular attention to thoughts and feelings. Judges the novels to be "unabashedly romantic." Considers her sense of language, unpublished writings, and creative process. Notes ways in which Philip Larkin influenced her work.

6 HOLT, HAZEL. "Philip Larkin and Barbara Pym: Two Quiet People." In *Philip Larkin: The Man and His Work.* Edited by Dale Salwak. London: Macmillan; Iowa City: University of Iowa Press, pp. 59-68.

Memoir of the friendship between Pym and Philip Larkin. During her period of neglect, "Philip encouraged and sustained her, partly by writing to her about the work she had in hand, taking her seriously, as one writer to another and, very practically, putting her in touch, with personal recommendations, with those publishers that he knew."

7 KNAPP, MONA. "Fiction: English." *World Literature Today* 63 (Winter):101.

Review of *Civil to Strangers and Other Writings.* Finds Pym's unmistakable voice in *Civil to Strangers. Gervase and Flora* is "memorable." The four short stories are excellent. *So Very Secret* is unconvincing.

8 LIDDELL, ROBERT. *A Mind at Ease: Barbara Pym and Her Novels.* London: Peter Owen, 143 pp.

Draws on his fifty years of friendship with Pym to write a critical survey of those works (through *Crampton Hodnet*) "which were prepared by herself for publication." Divides his study into three parts: "The Early Years," "The 'Canon,' " and "The Later Years." Considers the attention she gave to her characters' domestic and emotional lives, examines the reasons for her revival in popularity, and guides the reader through her novels, explaining which ones are or are not successful and why. Also corrects errors by critics and dilutes the common misconception that Pym is a modern-day Jane Austen.

9 PILGRIM, ANNE C. "Teaching the Novels of Barbara Pym and Jane Austen." *Barbara Pym Newsletter* 4 (December):12.

Reports on experience teaching a thirteen-week course covering five novels of Jane Austen and four of Pym. Includes a course description.

10 SADLER, LYNN VEACH. "Anita Brookner's Dons: Literature as the Way for a Woman in *A Start in Life* and *Providence*." *Barbara Pym Newsletter* 4 (December):1.

Like the heroines of Pym, Brookner's "live life at a reduced level" and relate to literature in a way reminiscent of Margaret Drabble's heroines.

11 WELD, ANNETTE FORKER. "Barbara Pym and the Novel of Manners." Ph.D. dissertation, University of Rochester, 375 pp.

Examines the conventions of the novel of manners as reflected in Pym's twelve autobiographical novels. "Closely bound by the constraints of economics, social class, and ethical behavior, the genre in Pym's hands reflects her debt to previous practitioners and her continuation and expansion of this conservative form." Considers early unpublished manuscripts as the "testing ground" for later works. Pym adds to the usual conventions "an unarticulated feminism, an ironic wit, and a firmly detailed documentation of the world as she saw it."

12 WHITNEY, CAROL WILKINSON. " 'Women Are So Terrified These Days': Fear between the Sexes in the World of Barbara Pym." *Essays in Literature* 16 (Spring):71-84.

Explores the relationship between the sexes in all twelve novels.

1990

1 BROTHERS, BARBARA. "Love, Marriage, and Manners in the Novels of Barbara Pym." In *Reading and Writing Women's Lives: A*

Study of the Novel of Manners. Edited by Bege K. Bowers and Barbara Brothers. Ann Arbor and London: UMI Research Press, pp. 153-70.

Considers all of Pym's novels within tradition of the novel of manners, but focuses on *Jane and Prudence* because "it specifically examines love, family, marriage, and work through the expectations and fantasies of women, counterpointing the past and the present, the 'young' and the middle-aged, the married and the unmarried, village social life and the city's office life, and the world of men and the world of women." Assesses the relationship between societal and literary conventions as well as literary, feminist, and general political concerns.

2 COOLEY, MASON. *The Comic Art of Barbara Pym.* New York: AMS Press, 276 pp.

Places Pym in the line of the great comic writers from Molière to Beckett. Her comedy ranges from "a witty display of slippage and incongruity in language and behavior (high comedy) to clowning and visual jokes (farce). In mood, it changes over the course of her career from hilarity to gravity." Thus her novels "are not tales of sadness and defeat but of a tenacious will to find sustenance and even enjoyment in the most unpromising circumstances."

3 GRIFFIN, BARBARA. "Order and Disruption in *Some Tame Gazelle.*" *Barbara Pym Newsletter* 5 (June):2-4.

Considers the degree to which disruption "emanates from Henry, is precipitated by the departure of Agatha, and is experienced by Belinda."

4 HOLT, HAZEL. *A Lot to Ask: A Life of Barbara Pym.* London: Macmillan. 308 pp.

Draws from interviews, journals and diaries, letters, and her close friendship with the author. Arranged chronologically. Her purpose: "to try to put Barbara into her own setting, to define the manners and mores of the social scene around her, . . . and to show how her books were moulded by her life, as well as the other way round." Avoids wherever possible repeating material that appeared in *A Very Private Eye.* Reprinted: 1991.1.

5 MOSELEY, MERRITT, and PAMELA J. NICKLESS. "Pym's Homosexuals." *Barbara Pym Newsletter* 5 (June):5-8.

Consider what homosexual men in Pym's novels have in common and what their treatment tells us about heterosexuals. "Man's weakness becomes his strength, and the homosexual becomes an interesting sort of noncombatant or double agent in the war of the sexes."

6 ____. "The State of Letters: A Few Words about Barbara Pym." *Sewanee Review* 98 (Winter):75-87.

Seeks to explain the source of Pym's appeal. Discusses her consistency, or recurrent features (unmarried women, Anglican church, English literature, anthropology, weak men), but the main reasons for her growing reputation and the reasons why people should read her are literary and aesthetic: her "creation of a little world," her "tough and absolutely clear-eyed realism," her high comedy, and her "perception of what is 'suitable.'" "It is what she does within her little world that makes Pym rewarding reading; her special voice, soft, firm, knowing, delicately humorous, just a bit acerbic, which illuminates these bits and makes them live."

7 SADLER, LYNN VEACH. *Anita Brookner*. Boston: Twayne, 165 pp., *passim*.

Notes similarities and differences between the life and work of Brookner and Pym. Both feature heroines who relate to the characters in literature, live as observers rather than participants, and concern themselves with moral issues.

8 STRAUSS-NOLL, MARY THERESE. "Barbara Pym's Favorites." *Barbara Pym Newsletter* 5 (June):9-13.

Considers what Pym's favorite characters have in common. "Perhaps Barbara Pym admired Leonora and the other proud heroines because, unlike her, they are not so deeply hurt when their romances end. Their vanity somewhat protects them from the pain of unrequited love. They do not suffer like the more vulnerable romantics: Belinda, Mildred, Dulcie, and Barbara Pym."

1991

1 BIXLER, FRANCES. "Female Narrative Structure in Barbara Pym's *Excellent Women*." *Barbara Pym Newsletter* 5 (January):2-6.

A reluctance to publish Pym's novels from 1961 to 1978 is linked to editors' "inability to read and value novels cast in female narrative form." In *Excellent Women,* for example, "a model of female narratology expands the reader's expectations and enriches the appreciation of the interpenetrating cycles which crowd the novel. . . . Her 'olden women' become interesting, vibrant human beings who meet life with zest and good humor. The interconnectedness of the lives of all the characters reflects the interconnectedness of human life. We are all, in a sense, 'olden women' if we care about and pay attention to our relationships with other people."

2 HOLT, HAZEL. *A Lot to Ask: A Life of Barbara Pym.* New York: Dutton, 308 pp.
Reprint of 1990.3.

Index

Abel, Betty, 1984.1
Ableman, Paul, 1978.1
Abley, Mark, 1984.2
"Absorbing and Satisfying,"
1977.14
Academic Question, An, 1985.27;
1986.1, 6, 7-8, 12, 14-16,
18-28, 31, 33-45, 47-48,
50-55, 57-58; 1987.15, 17-
18, 28, 36, 45-47; 1988.4,
7, 15, 33; 1989.1, 5, 11-12;
1990.1, 3
"*Academic Question* by Barbara
Pym, *An,*" 1986.21
"Aces in the Lively Pack," 1986.29
"Acid Humour from Angus,"
1980.46
Ackley, Katherine Anne, 1988.1;
1989.1
Ackroyd, Peter, 1978.2; 1982.1;
1984.3
Adams, Phoebe-Lou, 1985.1
Adamson, Lesley, 1977.1
"Address Given by the Rev.
William Jarvis . . .,"
1984.62
"Adult Fiction," (J. Brosnahan),
1985.15; (D. Donavin),

1986.20; (A. Kempf),
1986.35
"Ah, What Pym Can Do with a
Meager Plot," 1983.43
Alabaster, Carol, 1982.2
Allen, Bruce, 1981.1; 1982.3-4;
1983.1
"Amour of Lady to the Mannerly
Born," 1982.67
Anita Brookner, 1990.7
"Anita Brookner's Dons:
Literature as the Way for
a Woman in *A Start in
Life* and *Providence,*"
1989.10
"Announcement," 1980.1
"Annual *Biography* Evaluative
Survey, The," 1985.63
"Another Day, Another Pym's
Oates," 1987.15
"Anthropologist of the English
Middle Class, An,"
1982.33
"Approaching Height of
Novelist's Art!," 1978.60
Ardener, Edwin, 1986.4
"Art of Making Routine Lives
Absorbing, The," 1980.30

137

"High Comedy – Deftly Hidden,"
1980.25
"High Farce in North Oxford,"
1985.24
"High Spirit," 1984.21
Hildebrand, Holly, 1980.43;
1984.59
Hill, Rosemary, 1985.33
Hill, Susan, 1984.60
Hills, C.A.R., 1987.18
Hinerfeld, Susan Slocum, 1978.29;
1979.13
"Hissing Tea-urns and Sensuous
Hearts," 1987.27
Hitchcock, Alfred, 1987.9
"Holiday Gift Books," 1984.10
"Holiday Reading: Fiction,"
1978.7; 1985.6
Holloway, David, 1955.1
Holt, Hazel, 1983.49; 1984.12;
1985.27; 1986.30; 1987.19-
20; 1988.14; 1989.6;
1990.4, 1991.2
"Home Front: Barbara Pym in
Oswestry, 1939-1941,
The," 1988.14
Hooper, Brad, 1987.21
Hooper, William Bradley,
1980.44; 1981.19; 1982.37;
1983.32
Horan, David, 1986.29
Hospital, Janette T., 1978.30
"How Are the Mighty
Fallen – According to the
Critics," 1977.7
"How Barbara Pym Was
Rediscovered after 16
Years Out in the Cold,"
1977.24
"How Could I Have Waited So
Long, Miss Pym?,"
1984.31

"How Mundane and Compelling,"
1977.23
"How Pleasant to Know Miss
Pym," 1971.1; 1987.44
Howard, Philip, 1978.31
Howe, Pamela, 1984.61
Howell, Georgina, 1986.30
Hudson, Christopher, 1985.34
Hugh-Jones, Siriol, 1961.2
Hughes, David, 1977.16
Hughes, Riley, 1957.5
"Humourous and Gentle Country
Loves," 1983.40
Huth, Angela, 1987.22
Huxley, Aldous, *Crome Yellow,*
1988.5, 33; *Point
Counterpoint,* 1988.33;
Those Barren Leaves,
1988.33

" 'I Don't Need Anybody,' and
Other Illusions," 1979.17
"If You Don't Know Barbara Pym
. . .," 1983.35
"Illiterations," 1989.4
"Image of the Indexer, The?,"
1985.12
"Importance of Connecting, The,"
1987.3
"In a Minor Key," 1986.28
"In Brief," 1983.22, 71
"In Praise of Excellent Women,"
1983.24
"In Print," 1982.53; 1984.88
"In Short: Fiction," 1985.18
*Independent Women: The
Function of Gender in the
Novels of Barbara Pym,*
1988.23
"Index This One under 'D' – for
'Delightful,' " 1983.61
"Indexer Observes, An," 1988.19